# AINSLEY HARRIOTT'S
# GOURMET
# EXPRESS

This book is published to accompany the television series *Gourmet Express* which was first broadcast in 2000. The series was produced by BBC Birmingham.
Executive Editor: Franny Moyle
Series Producer: Sara Kozak
Director: Stuart Bateup

Published by BBC Worldwide Ltd,
80 Wood Lane, London W12 0TT

First published 2000
Reprinted 2000, 2001, 2002
This paperback edition first published 2002
© Ainsley Harriott 2000
The moral right of the author has been asserted.

Recipes developed and written in association with Silvana Franco
Studio photographs by Gus Filgate
© BBC Worldwide Ltd 2000
Location photography by Craig Easton
© BBC Worldwide Ltd 2000

ISBN 0 563 55179 8 hardback edition
ISBN 0 563 48826 3 paperback edition

Commissioning Editor: Nicky Copeland
Project Editor: Rachel Brown
Cover Art Director: Pene Parker
Book Art Director: Lisa Pettibone
Designer: John Calvert
Production Controller: Kenneth McKay
Food stylist: Silvana Franco assisted by Sharon Hearne
Props stylist: Penny Markham

Set in Eurostile and Humanist
Printed and bound in Great Britain by Butler & Tanner Ltd, Frome, Somerset
Colour origination by Radstock Reproductions Ltd
Jacket printed by Lawrence Allen Ltd

All the spoon measurements in this book are level unless otherwise stated.
A tablespoon is 15 ml; a teaspoon is 5 ml. Follow one set of measurements when preparing any of the recipes. Do not mix metric with imperial.
All eggs used in the recipes are medium sized.
All vegetables should be peeled unless the recipe says otherwise.

# CONTENTS

# INTRODUCTION

If you've had a hard day working at home, in the office, or looking after the kids, there's always another job that awaits you – cooking an evening meal.

For an instant quick fix, you could order a take-away, but these meals are often unappetizing, quite pricey and not that nutritious. So before you pick up the phone, have a look at the wonderful recipes in *Gourmet Express*, which can be prepared in hardly any time at all. The book is full of interesting, easy-to-make meals that have the right balance of colour, texture and flavour and taste great.

Fast food, as we know it in Britain, can often be disappointing, unlike other countries, where there is wonderful street food. Having been inspired by those foods while on my travels around the globe, I've included a whole chapter on snacks and hand-held food. Just wait till you try my Celtic Samosas, NYC Foolproof Falafels, Finger-lickin' Chicken, Wrap and Roll Hot Dogs and the new nibble on the block – Nori-rolled Sushi.

If you're in the mood for soup, this book spoils you for choice. I've created some delightful, quick and healthy soups for every occasion, plus some great starters that feed the eyes and totally satisfy the tastebuds.

But if you're up for doing a bit of preparation in advance, there's a whole feast of recipes that you can have ready to pop into the oven at a moment's notice for a delicious family supper. Try Super Shepherd's Pie, Ocean Cheese and Potato Pie, or how about a Cheeky Chicken Tikka Masala?

There are lots more great chicken, fish and meat dishes, and some really excellent vegetarian meals that will make you more than happy to go without your usual portion of meat.

For those of you who sometimes get stuck thinking about what to serve with a main course, there's a chapter on side orders and hot breads that will give you plenty of mouth-watering ideas. And don't forget to dip into the sauces and relishes section for some interesting flourishes.

Finally, the chapter on sweet bites and drinks introduces you to new ways of satisfying your sweet tooth. Just try my terrific Portuguese Custard Tarts, Banana Splits with Warm Choco-fudge Sauce, or a Simple Saffron Kulfi – naughty but all very, very nice.

Food has never been more exciting or inspiring than it is today, and we can now get fresh produce from all over the world in our local shops and supermarkets. Hooray! In *Gourmet Express* I've combined lots of those fresh ingredients with store-cupboard essentials, an approach that fits in with the busy modern lifestyle. You'll be amazed at what you can knock up with a few potatoes, some bacon and a can of crabmeat. Just a handful of tomatoes opens up all sorts of exciting culinary prospects, and with a packet of pasta, some chorizo sausage and a few Italian cheeses, Mediterranean food can come into your kitchen with little effort and loads of taste. So remember to stock up on those store-cupboard goodies and you'll never be short of ideas at meal times – especially with *Gourmet Express* by your side.

Happy smelly cooking,

# Sage and onion bhajis

Genuine bhajis are made with gram flour, from chick peas. I've decided to go for a bit of a cheat's version by using regular white flour and getting the yellow colour from turmeric. I've made them even more English by adding the classic onion sidekick, sage, and it really tastes fantastic – especially with a good dollop of Maddie's Mango Chutney (page 134) or Lovely Tomato Chutney (page 138).

**PREPARATION: 10 minutes  COOKING TIME: 5 minutes**

## SERVES 2

50 g (2 oz) self-raising flour

¼ teaspoon ground turmeric

½ red chilli, finely chopped

10 sage leaves, shredded

¼ teaspoon salt

1 onion, about 100 g (4 oz), sliced

vegetable oil, for frying

## METHOD

**1** Place the flour, turmeric, chilli, sage and salt in a bowl. Add enough water – about 5 tablespoons – to form a very thick batter. Stir in the onion.

**2** Heat 5 cm (2 inches) of oil in a wok or deep frying-pan and carefully drop the mixture into it using 2 tablespoons – 1 to scoop up the batter and the other to ease it into the oil (you might have to do this in batches). Cook for 4–5 minutes, turning occasionally, until golden brown and cooked through. Drain on kitchen paper and serve warm.

# Celtic samosas

Samosas are one of my all-time favourite snacks, especially straight from the pan. I vary the filling to match my vegetable rack but I've always got a few potatoes knocking around and some peas in the freezer. My son, Jimmy, calls these 'Celtic' samosas because they're green and white inside. They're fantastic with a spoonful of Maddie's Mango Chutney (page 134).

**PREPARATION: 40 minutes + 30 minutes resting  COOKING TIME: 10 minutes**

## SERVES 4

250 g (9 oz) plain flour

2 teaspoons baking powder

½ teaspoon salt

large pinch ground turmeric

40 g (1½ oz) unsalted butter, chilled and diced

**FOR THE FILLING**

2 tablespoons vegetable oil

1 small onion, finely chopped

2 garlic cloves, finely chopped

1 red chilli, seeded and finely chopped

350 g (12 oz) floury potatoes, cubed and boiled

75 g (3 oz) frozen peas, thawed

1 teaspoon ground cumin

salt

2 tablespoons chopped fresh coriander

vegetable oil, for deep-frying

## METHOD

**1** Sift the flour, baking powder, salt and turmeric into a bowl. Using your fingers, rub the butter into the flour until the mixture resembles breadcrumbs. Stir in about 150 ml (¼ pint) of water to make a soft dough. Knead well for a few minutes, then roll into 8 balls. Cover with a damp cloth and set aside for 30 minutes.

**2** Heat the oil in a large frying-pan and cook the onion, garlic and chilli for 3–4 minutes until softened and golden. Add the potatoes, mashing down roughly with a fork. Add the peas, cumin and salt to taste; remove from the heat and stir in the coriander.

**3** Heat about 5 cm (2 inches) of oil in a wok or deep-frying-pan. Meanwhile, roll out each piece of dough into a 10 cm (4 inch) round. Spoon an eighth of the potato mixture into the centre of each round. Moisten the edge of each round with a little water, then fold over the dough to enclose the filling, pressing the edges to seal, then gently flatten out each samosa. Fry the samosas in batches for about 2 minutes, turning until crisp and golden brown. Drain on kitchen paper and eat warm.

# Hot crispy
# Cajun chicken sandwich

This is one of my favourite ever late-night snacks. I vary the ingredients, depending on what's in the fridge, but all you really need is a skin-on chicken breast and a couple of slices of bread, then make up the trimmings as you go along. Other good things to put in a hot chicken sandwich include sliced gherkins, grainy mustard, sweet chilli sauce, sliced cheese or soft cheese with a shake of Tabasco.

**PREPARATION: 10 minutes  COOKING TIME: 15 minutes**

## SERVES 1

1 boneless, skin-on chicken breast

1 teaspoon Cajun seasoning, or ½ teaspoon Chinese five-spice powder and a pinch of cayenne pepper

salt and freshly ground black pepper

juice of ½ lemon (optional)

50 g (2 oz) mild blue cheese

1 tablespoon mayonnaise

4 cherry tomatoes, halved, or 1 small tomato, sliced

1 salad onion, sliced, or a few dice of raw onion

handful of salad leaves, if available

2 slices of bread

## METHOD

**1** Season the chicken with spice, salt and pepper. Cook skin-side down in a non-stick frying-pan for 5 minutes so the skin is nicely brown and crispy, then turn and cook for about another 4 minutes until cooked through but still moist and juicy. Now squeeze over a little lemon juice – a shake or two will do.

**2** While the chicken is cooking mash together the blue cheese and mayonnaise.

**3** Layer the salad ingredients on top of one of the slices of bread and top with the moist chicken followed by the blue cheese mayo. Sandwich together with the remaining bread and eat warm.

**TRY THIS:** Use different types of bread – French bread or pitta is equally delicious.

# NYC foolproof falafel
## with yoghurt drizzle

Real falafel have to be made with dried chick peas because the texture given by canned ones is just too soft. I've cooked many versions in the past and this is an authentic recipe – just pop a few falafel into a warmed pitta, top with a drizzle of yoghurt dressing and a pickled chilli and you'll get a snack that tastes every bit as good as one you'd buy on a New York street corner.

**PREPARATION: 15 minutes + overnight soaking  COOKING TIME: 15 minutes**

## SERVES 4-6 (makes 16 falafel)

225 g (8 oz) dried chick peas, soaked overnight in water

1 teaspoon salt

1 teaspoon baking powder

1 teaspoon cumin seeds

1 teaspoon ground coriander

½ teaspoon cayenne pepper

1 garlic clove, crushed

2 tablespoons chopped fresh parsley

juice of ½ lemon

vegetable oil for frying

pitta bread and natural yoghurt, to serve

## METHOD

**1** Drain the chick peas and place in a food processor with the salt, baking powder, cumin, coriander, cayenne, garlic, parsley and lemon juice. Whizz until very finely chopped but not puréed. (If you have time, set the mixture aside for a couple of hours so that the flavours can mingle, but it's not imperative.)

**2** Heat 5 cm (2 inches) of oil in a deep frying-pan or wok.

**3** Using wet hands, shape the mixture into 16 balls, then flatten slightly into patties. Deep-fry in batches for about 4 minutes, turning occasionally until browned. Remove with a slotted spoon and drain on kitchen paper.

**4** Serve 3 or 4 falafel inside a warm pitta bread pocket, with a drizzle of yoghurt over.

# Olé nachos Mexicanos

This incredibly quick snack is easy to make at any time, but especially when my mates pop round to watch the footie: 'Did you see him save that?' Olé!

**PREPARATION: 5 minutes  COOKING TIME: 5 minutes**

## SERVES 2

150 g bag tortilla chips

200 g can chopped tomatoes

salt and freshly ground black pepper

4 salad onions, thinly sliced

2 mild red chillies, thinly sliced

50 g (2 oz) Gruyère or Cheddar, grated

150 g carton soured cream

## METHOD

**1** Pre-heat the grill to medium. Tip the tortilla chips into a large heatproof dish. Spoon over the chopped tomatoes and season lightly. Scatter over the salad onions, chillies and finally the cheese.

**2** Place under the grill for 5 minutes until the cheese starts to melt and bubble. Serve warm, with the soured cream added to each mouthwatering mouthful.

**TRY THIS:** Take a look at the wide selection of tortilla chips now available in your local supermarket. Choosing a variety such as the 'fiery hot' or 'cooling soured cream' can really add an extra dimension to your nachos. And a sprinkling of pickled jalapeño chillies, if you can find them, add an authentic spicy bite to this great quick snack.

# Tempura prawn
## and vegetable treat

Tempura is a Japanese dish of battered, deep-fried slices of vegetable and prawns. There are lots of different ways of making tempura batter. I've simplified the process by dusting the vegetables in cornflour before dipping them in frothy egg white – it gives a crisp, golden result.

**PREPARATION: 20 minutes  COOKING TIME: 15 minutes**

## SERVES 4

**FOR THE DIPPING SAUCE**

100 ml (3½ fl oz) vegetable stock

4 tablespoons soy sauce

1 tablespoon sweet chilli sauce

2 tablespoons dry sherry

2.5 cm (1 inch) root ginger, finely grated

sprigs of coriander, to garnish

**FOR THE TEMPURA**

vegetable oil, for deep-frying

4 tablespoons cornflour

½ teaspoon salt

3 large egg whites

500 g (1 lb 2 oz) mixed vegetables, e.g. whole baby spinach leaves, halved mushrooms, sliced sweet potato, courgette, aubergine, red pepper

12 large, raw peeled prawns, tail section left intact

## METHOD

**1** To make the dipping sauce place the stock, soy sauce, chilli sauce, sherry and ginger in a large pan and bring to the boil. Simmer for 5 minutes.

**2** Meanwhile, heat 4 cm (1½ inches) of oil in a wok. Mix together the cornflour and salt. Whisk together the egg whites and 4 tablespoons of very cold water until light and frothy. Dust the vegetable pieces and prawns with the cornflour, then dip in the frothy egg; deep-fry in batches for 3–4 minutes until golden. Drain on kitchen paper.

**3** Pour the sauce into small bowls. Pile the vegetables on to serving plates and serve immediately with the dipping sauce.

# Hot-smoked salmon pâté
## with toasted bagels

This is a twist on the classic New York smoked salmon and cream cheese bagel. Hot-smoked salmon is available from supermarkets and delicatessens and by mail order from various fish-smokeries.

**PREPARATION: 15 minutes  COOKING TIME: 5 minutes**

## SERVES 4

1 tablespoon olive oil

4 salad onions, thinly sliced

500 g (1 lb 2 oz) hot-smoked salmon, skinned and boned

250 g carton soft cheese

1 teaspoon creamed horseradish

dash of Tabasco

freshly ground black pepper

4 bagels

knob of butter

## METHOD

1  Heat the oil in a pan and sauté the salad onions for 1 minute. Flake in the fish, then beat well, cooking for a further minute or two. Remove from the heat – if the mixture gets too hot, allow to cool slightly.

2  Add the soft cheese, horseradish, Tabasco and black pepper, and mix together until well combined.

3  Split open the bagels and lightly toast. Butter generously and serve with the hot-smoked salmon pâté and, if you like, a sprinkling of thinly sliced spring onion.

**CHEF'S TIP:** The hot-smoked salmon has a naturally salty flavour, so don't add extra.

Hot-smoked salmon pâté with toasted bagels

# Webby cheese
## and Parma flatbread

This is a wonderful casual snack that's quick and always impressive, especially with a bowl of chillied black olives. I love to use Italian Fontina cheese for this as it goes all gooey, webby and stretchy as it melts. Other good cheeses to use are mozzarella, Gruyère or even good old Cheddar.

**PREPARATION: 5 minutes  COOKING TIME: 5 minutes**

## SERVES 1

1 teaspoon Dijon mustard

2 x 20 cm (8 inch) flour tortillas

75 g (5 oz) Fontina, finely grated

2 slices Parma ham

freshly ground black pepper

1 teaspoon vegetable oil

## METHOD

**1** Smear the mustard on to one of the tortillas and scatter over the grated cheese, ham and plenty of black pepper. Place the second tortilla on top and press together firmly.

**2** Brush a large non-stick frying-pan with the oil. Cook the sandwich for a minute or so on each side until crisp and well browned and molten inside. Cut into wedges or squares and eat warm.

**TRY THIS:** If you fancy pushing the boat out, layer fresh basil or rocket in with the cheese and ham.

# Kofta rolls with chilli-yoghurt

These tasty little koftas are so much better than a lot of the kebabs you can buy from fast food restaurants – and, what's more, they're much better for you too. The chilli-yoghurt has a wonderful fresh flavour and really sets the whole thing off with a bang.

**PREPARATION: 15 minutes  COOKING TIME: 15 minutes**

## SERVES 4

450 g (1 lb) minced lamb

1 small onion, finely chopped

1 tablespoon chopped fresh mint

1 tablespoon chopped fresh parsley

2 teaspoons chopped fresh rosemary

½ teaspoon each mixed spice, ground coriander and ground cumin

salt and freshly ground black pepper

4 flour tortillas

1 red onion, thinly sliced into rings

### FOR THE CHILLI-YOGHURT

300 g (11 oz) Greek yoghurt

3 red chillies, seeded and finely chopped

2 tablespoons chopped fresh coriander

2 garlic cloves, crushed

juice of 1 lime

pinch of caster sugar

salt and freshly ground black pepper

## METHOD

**1** Pre-heat the grill to high. Mix together the lamb, onion, herbs and spices and season with salt and pepper. Divide the mixture into four and, using your fingers, squeeze it around skewers to form long sausage shapes.

**2** Grill the kofta kebabs for 10–12 minutes, turning occasionally, until well browned but still a little pink in the centre.

**3** Make the dip: combine the yoghurt, chillies, coriander, garlic, lime juice and sugar, and season to taste.

**4** Briefly warm the tortillas for a few seconds on each side in a dry, non-stick frying-pan, or for 10 seconds in a microwave, to make them soft and pliable. Place a kebab in the centre of each tortilla, pulling it off the skewer. Scatter over the onion rings, drizzle over the chilli-yoghurt and serve.

# Nori-rolled sushi
## with soy dipping sauce

Sushi is high fashion at the moment – not only is it very healthy, but it tastes great too. I get asked loads of questions about it, so I've included this classic recipe that is delicious and not too challenging. You really need a proper sushi-rolling mat to make this kind of sushi, but they can be bought cheaply from oriental stores.

**PREPARATION: 30 minutes  COOKING TIME: 15 minutes + cooling**

## SERVES 4

200 g (7 oz) Japanese rice

4 tablespoons white vinegar, such as rice vinegar or white wine vinegar

1 tablespoon caster sugar

1 teaspoon salt

½ cucumber, seeded

1 avocado

175 g (6 oz) fresh tuna or salmon

4 sheets nori seaweed

1 teaspoon wasabi paste (Japanese horseradish)

pickled ginger, to serve

Soy Dipping Sauces (page 142), to serve

## METHOD

**1** Begin by cooking the rice. Wash it well in warm water, then place in a pan. Cover with water so that it comes 2 cm (¾ inch) above the rice. Cover and cook gently for 12 minutes, or until the rice is tender and the water has been absorbed.

**2** Meanwhile, mix together the vinegar, sugar and salt and set aside to dissolve. As soon as the rice is cooked, stir the vinegar mixture into it and leave to cool completely.

**3** Cut the cucumber, avocado and fish into batons.

**4** Halve the nori sheets and place one half horizontally on the rolling mat. Spread 2–3 tablespoons of the rice mixture on the seaweed, leaving a 1 cm (½ inch) margin on the edge furthest from you.

**5** Spread a tiny amount of the wasabi across the centre of the rice, then place a row of cucumber and avocado or fish across the centre. Roll up so the join is on the bottom of the roll. Continue to make rolls, alternating the ingredients so that some contain just fish and others contain cucumber and avocado.

**6** Trim the ends of the rolls with a sharp knife, then cut each into six pieces. Transfer to serving dishes and place a pile of pickled ginger with each. Serve with one of my Soy Dipping Sauces (page 142) – simply delicious and heavenly healthy.

# Wrap and roll hot dogs
## with mustard onion relish

Serving good old hot dogs in a tortilla wrap brings them right back up to date, but you can always slot them into soft finger rolls if you prefer. So come on, wrap or roll, the choice is yours.

**PREPARATION: 10 minutes  COOKING TIME: 20 minutes**

## SERVES 4

4 jumbo pork sausages

2 tablespoons olive oil

1 large red onion, thinly sliced

1 garlic clove, finely chopped

1 teaspoon yellow mustard seeds

salt and freshly ground black pepper

4 flour tortillas

Maddie's Mango Chutney (page 134), to serve

## METHOD

**1** Pre-heat the oven to 200°C/400°F/Gas 6. Place the sausages on a baking sheet and roast for about 20 minutes until cooked through and rich golden brown.

**2** Meanwhile, heat the olive oil in a small frying-pan and cook the onion and garlic over a low heat for 10 minutes or so until soft and golden. Add the mustard seeds and cook for another couple of minutes, then season to taste with salt and pepper.

**3** Place the tortilla wraps in the warm oven for a couple of minutes just to soften them up and make them easier to roll. Place a sausage in the centre of each wrap and top with a spoonful of the chutney and the mustard onion relish. Roll up and serve warm.

# Late-night egg and
# sausage-sizzle sarnie

When you're feeling hungry – day or night – the thought of a hot, juicy, eggy sandwich is enough to make the hair on the back of your neck stand up – what hair, Ainsley?

**PREPARATION: 5 minutes  COOKING TIME: 15 minutes**

## SERVES 1

2 teaspoons olive oil

1 pork sausage, cut into 1 cm (½ inch) pieces

2 salad onions, thinly sliced

2 eggs

2 tablespoons milk

salt and freshly ground black pepper

2 slices white bread

small knob of butter at room temperature

1 tablespoon Lovely Tomato Chutney (page 138) or brown sauce

## METHOD

**1** Heat the oil in a 20 cm (8 inch) frying-pan and cook the sausage for 5 minutes until golden. Add the salad onions and cook for a further minute or two.

**2** Beat together the eggs, milk and some seasoning and pour over the sausage. Cook for a couple of minutes on each side until set and golden.

**3** Butter the slices of bread and slide the omelette on to the unbuttered side of one of the pieces of bread. Top with the remaining slice of bread, butter-side up.

**4** Cook the sandwich in the pan for 2–3 minutes on each side until crisp and golden brown. Cut in half and eat warm with the chutney or sauce.

# Harissa-rubbed lamb
## in charred pitta

I use lamb fillet for this dish because it's really tender, although you could use neck fillet, which is cheaper, but a little fatty (not me, the lamb). Harissa works fantastically well with lamb, though if that's not available, you could use another chilli paste. I find hummus a really good accompaniment to the lamb: you can buy it ready-made from supermarkets, or why not make your own? See my recipe for Coriander Hummus on page 33.

**PREPARATION: 15 minutes  COOKING TIME: 15 minutes**

## SERVES 4

1 tablespoon harissa or other chilli paste or sauce

juice of 1 lemon

2 tablespoons chopped fresh mint

½ teaspoon sea salt

350 g (12 oz) lamb fillets

4 pitta breads

50 g (2 oz) fresh rocket

170 g carton fresh hummus or 1 quantity of Coriander Hummus (page 33)

lemon wedges, to garnish

## METHOD

**1** Mix together the harissa, lemon juice, chopped mint and sea salt. Add the lamb fillets, turning to coat in the mixture, and set aside to marinate for 10 minutes or so.

**2** Heat a chargrill pan for 2–3 minutes until hot. Add the lamb fillets and cook for 8–12 minutes until well browned but still a little pink in the centre; remove from the heat and allow to rest for 5 minutes to tenderize the meat. Warm the pitta in the same pan.

**3** Cut the pittas in half and fill each pocket with the rocket leaves.

**4** Diagonally slice the lamb into 1 cm (½ inch) thick slices and pack into the pitta. Top with a dollop of hummus and serve warm with lemon wedges for squeezing over.

# Coconut chicken satay pockets

Chicken fillets (the little pieces underneath regular breasts) are great for this dish because they're exactly the right size. I buy them from my local butcher, but larger supermarkets sell them in packets. If you can only get regular chicken breasts, cut them into 2 cm (¾ inch) wide strips, then bat them out with a rolling pin to flatten them slightly. The result is delicious and exquisite.

**PREPARATION: 15 minutes  COOKING TIME: 10 minutes**

## SERVES 4

200 g carton coconut cream

4 tablespoons crunchy peanut butter

2 tablespoons light soy sauce

1 tablespoon runny honey

few drops Tabasco sauce

25 g (1 oz) dry roast peanuts, roughly chopped

salt and freshly ground black pepper

250 g (9 oz) chicken fillets

4 mini naan breads, to serve

1 fresh lime, cut into wedges

## METHOD

1  Pre-heat the grill to high. Soak 4 bamboo skewers in hot water.

2  Place the coconut cream and peanut butter in a bowl and beat together until well blended. Stir in the light soy sauce, honey, Tabasco and peanuts, and season to taste. If the sauce is too thick, add a little water.

3  Pour the sauce into a shallow dish and add the chicken fillets, turning to coat them in the sauce. Thread on to the skewers and cook under the grill for 4 minutes on each side until cooked through and well browned.

4  Warm the naan breads under the grill, then split in half. Remove the chicken fillets from the skewers and push them into the naan breads. Squeeze over a little lime juice and enjoy

**TRY THIS:** If you want to serve the filled pockets with the remaining sauce, make sure you heat it thoroughly with a little water so you can drizzle it over the chicken.

# Melting mushroom
# Swiss burgers

For a truly sensational burger, jazz it up with a mouthwatering topping, such as the garlic mushrooms with melted Swiss cheese described here.

**PREPARATION: 15 minutes  COOKING TIME: 10 minutes**

## SERVES 4

500 g (1 lb 2 oz) lean beef mince

4 tablespoons chopped fresh parsley

1 egg yolk

salt and freshly ground black pepper

1 tablespoon sunflower oil

4 slices Gruyère, Emmenthal or other melty Swiss cheese

4 seeded burger buns and shredded lettuce, to serve

### FOR THE GARLIC MUSHROOMS

2 tablespoons olive oil

2 garlic cloves, crushed

250 g (9 oz) chestnut mushrooms, sliced

½ teaspoon cayenne pepper

## METHOD

**1** Mix together the mince, parsley, egg yolk and plenty of salt and pepper. Shape the mixture into 4 even-sized burgers.

**2** Brush the burgers with the sunflower oil and cook on a hot griddle or in a frying-pan for 3 minutes without turning.

**3** Meanwhile, heat the olive oil in a separate frying-pan and cook the garlic for 30 seconds. Add the mushrooms, cayenne and a little salt and cook for 2–3 minutes until softened and well browned.

**4** Turn the burgers and lay a slice of Swiss cheese on top of each. Cook for a few more minutes until the burger is well browned but still a little pink in the centre and the cheese is beginning to soften and melt.

**5** Scatter shredded lettuce over the base of each burger bun and top each with a melted Swiss cheese burger. Spoon over the garlic mushrooms, place the lid on top and serve immediately.

**TRY THIS:** I make a classic burger like this with pure beef, but mixing your minces can give you a really good result. Lamb is quite fatty but adds good flavour, so try half-and-half lamb and beef. Chicken and pork together and pork with sausage meat also combine to make great burgers, patties and meatballs as well as fillings for pasta dishes such as ravioli or cannelloni. Also, you could try replacing the burger buns with English muffins for a change.

# Parisian
## mustard sausage rolls

Fresh croissant dough is available in the chill cabinet of larger supermarkets. It's great rolled and cooked as on the packet instructions, but even better if filled with juicy sausages.

**PREPARATION: 10 minutes  COOKING TIME: 20 minutes**

## MAKES 6

1 tablespoon vegetable oil

6 pork sausages

1 x 240 g tube of chilled croissant dough

1 tablespoon Dijon mustard

1 egg yolk

pinch of salt

### FOR THE DIP

4 tablespoons tomato ketchup

2 teaspoons horseradish sauce

## METHOD

**1** Heat the oil in a large frying-pan and cook the sausages until nicely browned; allow to cool.

**2** Pre-heat the oven to 200°C/400°F/Gas 6. Open out the dough, then break along the markings to give six triangles. Smear a little mustard into the centre of each triangle, then place a sausage at the short, straight end and roll up towards the point.

**3** Arrange the sausage rolls on a baking sheet. Beat together the egg yolk and salt and brush over the dough. Bake for 10–12 minutes until puffed and golden brown.

**4** Meanwhile, mix together the ketchup and horseradish. Serve the sausage rolls warm with the dip.

# Finger-lickin' chicken

Well, this is my simple but very tasty version of that famous take-away chicken dish. I actually find it a lot easier to use the oven, as you cook the whole lot in one go rather than frying it in batches, and once it's in the oven you can leave it alone – until it arrives at the table, that is.

**PREPARATION: 10 minutes  COOKING TIME: 40 minutes**

## SERVES 4

1 medium chicken cut into 8 pieces, or 8 chicken drumsticks and thighs

1 tablespoon vegetable oil

5 tablespoons plain flour

1 tablespoon Cajun seasoning

1 teaspoon cayenne pepper

½ teaspoon salt

## METHOD

**1** Pre-heat the oven to 220°C/425°F/Gas 7. Rub the chicken skin with the oil. Place the flour, Cajun seasoning, cayenne pepper and salt in a large bowl and mix well together.

**2** Toss the chicken pieces in the flour until lightly coated. Place the chicken on a wire rack and sit the rack on a baking sheet. Cook the chicken for 35–45 minutes until cooked through with a good crispy skin; serve hot and eat with your fingers.

# No-cook oh so spring rolls

I buy rice paper discs from my local oriental grocers. They're really cheap and the best thing about them is that you just need to soak them in hot water before using, although they need to be handled carefully to avoid splits. Make sure you buy the savoury variety rather than those used for biscuits and sweets. These rolls are oh so scrummy.

**PREPARATION: 20 minutes**

## SERVES 4

7.5 x 15 cm (3 x 6 inch) rice paper wrappers

1 carrot, cut into matchsticks

10 cm (4 inch) piece cucumber cut into matchsticks

4 salad onions, shredded

1 teaspoon toasted sesame seeds

2 tablespoons hoisin sauce

350 g (12 oz) cooked chicken, shredded

## METHOD

**1** Place the rice paper wrappers in a heatproof bowl and cover with hot water; leave to soak for 5 minutes until soft and pliable.

**2** In a separate bowl, toss together the carrot, cucumber, salad onions and sesame seeds.

**3** Drain the rice papers on a clean tea towel and spread 1 teaspoon of hoisin sauce across the centre of each. Pile the vegetables and then the chicken on top.

**4** Fold two sides in, then roll up to make a neat cylindrical shape. Serve within an hour or two.

**CHEF'S TIP:** The spring rolls are not at their best if made up too far ahead of time. Instead, prepare the vegetables and the chicken, cover separately and chill until ready to use.

# Spiced, speckled
# tuna mayonnaise on rye

There are lots of different rye breads available. Pumpernickel can be quite strong and crumbly in the mouth, so I prefer to use a malted rye or a sourdough bread for this special sandwich. You can also serve these as open sandwiches – just garnish with a sprig of coriander and serve with a few nice, ripe cherry tomatoes and olives.

**PREPARATION: 10 minutes**

## SERVES 1

1 small can of tuna in brine, drained

1 shallot, very finely chopped

1 garlic clove, crushed

3 tablespoons mayonnaise

pinch of cayenne pepper

2 tablespoons chopped fresh coriander

salt and freshly ground black pepper

small knob of butter, at room temperature

2 slices light rye bread

50 g (2 oz) bag handcooked salted crisps

## METHOD

**1** Mix together the tuna, shallot, garlic, mayonnaise, cayenne and coriander and season to taste.

**2** Butter the bread, then spread over the tuna mixture. Smash the crisps into small pieces and scatter over the tuna. Grind over a little black pepper, top with the remaining slice of bread. Cut in half and eat immediately.

# Coriander hummus
## with crispy garlic pitta

Hummus is wonderful spread on crackers or chunks of warm bread, or scooped up with toasted crispy garlic pitta bread.

**PREPARATION: 10 minutes  COOKING TIME: 5 minutes**

## SERVES 6

2 garlic cloves, roughly chopped

2 mild red chillies, seeded and roughly chopped

large bunch fresh coriander, roughly chopped

2 x 420 g cans chick peas, drained

juice of 1 lime

4 tablespoons olive oil

salt and freshly ground black pepper

### FOR THE CRISPY GARLIC PITTA

3 tablespoons olive oil

2 garlic cloves, crushed

2 tablespoons chopped fresh parsley

4 white pitta breads

## METHOD

**1** Place the garlic, chillies and coriander in a food processor and whizz until finely chopped. Add the chick peas and whizz until well blended.

**2** With the motor running, squeeze in the lime juice and drizzle in the olive oil to make a fairly coarse paste. Season well to taste and spoon into a serving bowl.

**3** Meanwhile, mix together the olive oil, garlic and parsley and season. Heat one side of the pitta breads under a hot grill for about 1 minute until well browned.

**4** Turn over the bread, then use a knife to slash the softer surface 4–5 times without cutting through the bread. Brush with the herb and oil mixture and return to the grill until bubbling and toasted (about 1 minute).

**5** When cool, break into pieces and serve with the yummy hummus.

**CHEF'S TIP:** This is one of my favourite picnic recipes. Spoon the hummus into a lock-tight food bag and pack the pitta into an airtight box until you're ready to eat them. Don't forget to pack that crisp, chilled white wine.

# Prawn
## and chilli ginger cakes

These soft, fluffy fritters are delicious, especially when drizzled with my Sweet Chilli Sauce (page 143) or a squeeze of fresh lime juice.

**PREPARATION: 15 minutes  COOKING TIME: 10 minutes**

## SERVES 4 (makes 12)

2 thick slices white bread, crusts removed, about 100 g (4 oz)

250 g (9 oz) peeled raw prawns

1 green chilli, finely chopped

2.5 cm (1 inch) piece fresh root ginger, finely chopped

4 garlic cloves, finely chopped

1 tablespoon chopped fresh coriander

1 teaspoon salt

1 egg

vegetable oil for shallow-frying

baby lettuce leaves, to serve

## METHOD

**1** Place the bread in a bowl, cover with water, soak for about 10 seconds, then squeeze out the excess water. Place the drained bread in a food processor with the prawns, chilli, ginger, garlic, coriander, salt and egg. Pulse until well blended.

**2** Heat the oil and shallow-fry spoonfuls of the mixture for 2–3 minutes on each side until puffed and golden brown. Drain on kitchen paper and serve warm on a bed of baby lettuce leaves.

Prawn and chilli ginger cakes *with* Sweet chilli sauce

# Dimitri's festive feta triangles

This recipe brings back some wonderful memories of Greek holidays in Salonika – sunshine, sea and my mate Dimitri. The quantities given here will make lots of parcels, so they're perfect for serving as a starter when friends come over, or just for family nibbles. They're also great for picnics, and they freeze beautifully, too (see TRY THIS below).

**PREPARATION: 30 minutes  COOKING TIME: 10 minutes**

## MAKES 16

250 g (9 oz) feta cheese, crumbled

6 sun-dried tomatoes in oil, drained and chopped

150 g (5 oz) pitted black olives (preferably Kalamata), chopped

4 tablespoons chopped fresh parsley

2 tablespoons chopped fresh sage

½ teaspoon coarsely ground black pepper

1 tablespoon olive oil

8 sheets filo pastry, roughly 18 x 30 cm (7 x 12 inches)

50 g (2 oz) butter, melted

## METHOD

**1** Pre-heat the oven to 220°C/425°F/Gas 7. Mix together the feta, sun-dried tomatoes, olives, parsley, sage, pepper and olive oil.

**2** Cut each sheet of pastry in half lengthways to make long strips, roughly 9 cm (3½ inches) wide. Place a spoonful of the mixture at one end of each strip and fold the corner over diagonally. Fold over again to enclose the filling and continue down the strip to make a neat, triangular parcel.

**3** Transfer to a baking sheet, brush with melted butter and bake at the top of the oven for 8–10 minutes until golden brown. Serve warm.

**TRY THIS:** Arrange the cooked, cooled triangles on a tray and open-freeze for a couple of hours. Wrap loosely in freezer wrap and pack into a rigid plastic box or freezer bag and return to the freezer for up to one month. Defrost thoroughly before cooking.

For a nutty alternative, sprinkle a few sesame seeds on top of the triangles before baking.

# Char-grilled vegetables and hummus ciabatta

Grilling vegetables releases natural sugars, which gives them a lovely charred flavour. Slap them between two pieces of sun-dried tomato ciabatta bread, add a spreading of hummus and a sprinkling of rocket or basil and you really have a very exciting eating experience.

**PREPARATION: 10 minutes  COOKING TIME: 15 minutes**

## SERVES 2

1 courgette, sliced lengthways

1 red pepper, quartered lengthways and seeded

1 tablespoon olive oil

salt and freshly ground black pepper

1 ciabatta loaf

1 sun-dried tomato in oil, finely chopped

2 handfuls rocket or a few fresh basil leaves

4 tablespoons hummus

## METHOD

1 Brush the courgette and pepper pieces with oil, season and cook in a hot griddle pan or large frying-pan for 5–6 minutes on each side until softened, browned and a little charred.

2 Cut the ciabatta into 2 equal pieces, then split each half open.

3 Sprinkle the base of each half with the sun-dried tomato and scatter over the rocket or basil.

4 Arrange the char-grilled vegetables on top, then spoon over the hummus. Place the lid of the bread on top to form a sandwich, whack it in half and serve immediately.

**TRY THIS:** Why not try grilling other vegetables, such as aubergine, leeks, asparagus or strips of carrot?

# Tomato and feta bruschetta

Serve this snack and take a quick trip round the Med – 'bruschetta' is the Italian word for toasted bread, while rubbing the garlic over the top is very Spanish, and I've added feta and tomato for a Greek touch.

**PREPARATION: 15 minutes + resting time  COOKING TIME: 5 minutes**

## SERVES 4

250 g (9 oz) pomodorino or cherry tomatoes

200 g (7oz) feta cheese

small handful fresh mint leaves

small handful fresh basil

2–3 tablespoons olive oil

sea salt and freshly ground black pepper

1 ciabatta loaf

1 large garlic clove, unpeeled

## METHOD

**1** Place the tomatoes in a sturdy bowl, then use the end of a rolling pin to bash them and roughly flatten them open.

**2** Crumble or roughly dice the feta into the bowl. Roughly tear in the herbs, then add 2 tablespoons of olive oil and plenty of seasoning. Set aside for at least a couple of hours.

**3** Split the ciabatta in half lengthways, then cut each half widthways into 4 roughly equal-sized pieces. Drizzle the cut sides with a little olive oil and heat in a hot griddle pan or under a preheated grill until golden brown.

**4** Cut the garlic clove in half and rub the cut sides over the surface of the toasted bread; sprinkle lightly with salt. Pile the tomato mixture on top and serve – a little extra coarsely ground black pepper gives the bruschetta the perfect finish.

# Crispy crunchy
# sweetcorn fritters

Memories of my childhood come flooding back when I think of these delightful fritters. My late mother, Peppy, would always make these for a weekend treat, accompanied with black grilled tomatoes and honey bacon. Mmmm...

**PREPARATION: 5 minutes  COOKING TIME: 10 minutes**

## SERVES 4

420 g can creamed sweetcorn

2 salad onions, finely chopped

2 tablespoons chopped fresh parsley

4–5 heaped tablespoons cornflour

salt and freshly ground black pepper

vegetable oil, for frying

soured cream, to serve

## METHOD

**1** Mix together the corn, salad onions, parsley, cornflour and plenty of seasoning.

**2** Heat a little oil in a large frying-pan and cook large spoonfuls of the mixture for 2–3 minutes on each side until crisp and golden. Drain on kitchen paper and serve with a dollop of soured cream and a little freshly ground black pepper.

**TRY THIS:** Why not grill some streaky bacon until crisp and scatter on top of the soured cream?

# CHAPTER TWO SOUP TO GO

# Roasted tomato
## and crème fraîche soup

Roasting the tomatoes really intensifies the flavour – and it's still a very easy soup to make. I love to serve this with Mozzamary Garlic Bread (page 118).

**PREPARATION: 30 minutes  COOKING TIME: 45 minutes**

## SERVES 4

8 ripe tomatoes, halved

1 red onion, cut into quarters

1 head of garlic, halved horizontally

2 sprigs thyme

2 tablespoons olive oil

sea salt and freshly ground black pepper

1 litre (1¾ pints) hot vegetable stock

100 g (4 oz) crème fraîche

3 tablespoons chopped fresh parsley

warm bread, to serve

## METHOD

**1** Pre-heat the oven to 200°C/400°F/Gas 6. Place the tomatoes, red onion, garlic and thyme in a roasting tin and drizzle over the olive oil. Season generously and roast for 30 minutes until softened and a little charred.

**2** Remove the onions and garlic from the roasting tin and set aside. Pour half the stock over the tomatoes and return to the oven for 10 minutes.

**3** Meanwhile, slip the onions and garlic out of their papery skins and whizz in a food processor to form a paste.

**4** Remove the roasting tin from the oven, discard the thyme, then add the stock and tomatoes to the food processor, scraping up any residue with a wooden spoon.

**5** Strain the mixture into a clean pan and add the remaining stock and the crème fraîche. Heat gently and season to taste. Stir in the parsley, ladle into bowls and serve with warm crusty bread.

Roasted tomato and crème fraîche soup *with* Mozzamary garlic bread

# Butternut squash spiced soup

If you've not tried squash, this is a great way to enjoy it. Squash cooks down to a smooth purée, which makes for a lovely rich soup. I like to make this with butternut squash, which has great flavour, but you can use other squashes, or another delicious substitute is pumpkin.

**PREPARATION: 10 minutes  COOKING TIME: 40 minutes**

## SERVES 4

1 tablespoon olive oil

1 onion, finely chopped

1 kg (2 lb) diced squash or pumpkin

1 teaspoon cumin seeds

3 tablespoons curry paste

1 litre (1¾ pints) hot vegetable stock

275 ml carton double cream

3 tablespoons chopped fresh coriander

juice of ½ lemon

salt and freshly ground black pepper

warm naan bread, to serve

extra cream for swirling (optional but nice)

## METHOD

**1** Heat the oil in a large pan and cook the onion and squash or pumpkin over a gentle heat for 5–8 minutes until beginning to turn golden. Add the cumin seeds and cook for a further minute.

**2** Stir in the curry paste, pour over the hot stock, cover and simmer for 30 minutes until tender.

**3** Liquidize with a hand-held blender or push the mixture through a sieve. Return to the pan, stir in the cream and heat through gently. Stir in the coriander and squeeze in the lemon juice. Season with salt and pepper to taste. Ladle into bowls and serve with warm naan bread.

# Easy lentil supper soup

This delicious and substantial vegetarian soup is so easy and economical to make, and it's even better on day two. My late mother used to cook it slowly with a ham hock, so for you ham lovers, simply shred up some smoked ham or pancetta and add 5 minutes before serving.

**PREPARATION: 10 minutes  COOKING TIME: 35 minutes**

## SERVES 4

1 tablespoon olive oil

1 onion, finely chopped

2 carrots, finely diced

2 garlic cloves, finely chopped

1 red chilli, seeded and finely diced

1 teaspoon yellow mustard seeds

3 tomatoes, roughly diced

100 g (4 oz) red lentils

1.2 litres (2 pints) vegetable stock

juice of ½ lemon

salt and freshly ground black pepper

## METHOD

**1** Heat the oil in a large pan and cook the onion and carrots for about 3–4 minutes until beginning to soften. Add the garlic, chilli and mustard seeds and cook for a further couple of minutes.

**2** Stir in the tomatoes, lentils and stock and bring to the boil. Reduce the heat, cover and simmer gently for 30 minutes until the lentils are tender and easy to crush.

**3** Squeeze in the lemon juice, season with salt and pepper to taste. Ladle into warm bowls and serve.

# Hot and sour
## chicken and mushroom soup

Delicious hot and sour soups are all the rage at the moment. My recipe below is made with chicken, but you could also try making it with prawns, diced or minced pork, or just extra vegetables. Look out for frozen wontons and fish wontons in oriental stores or good supermarkets – the wontons make a great addition to the soup. Or serve the soup with Sesame Prawn Toasts (page 112).

**PREPARATION: 10 minutes  COOKING TIME: 15 minutes**

## SERVES 2

1 lemon grass stalk

600 ml (1 pint) hot chicken stock

4 boneless, skinless chicken thighs, diced

1–2 teaspoons Thai red curry paste

1 shallot, finely chopped

100 g (4 oz) shiitake mushrooms, sliced, or canned straw mushrooms, halved

2 teaspoons light muscovado sugar

2 teaspoons fish sauce

juice of 1 lemon

salt and freshly ground black pepper

1 salad onion, thinly sliced

1 red chilli, thinly sliced

handful of fresh coriander leaves

## METHOD

**1** Flatten the lemon grass stalk with a rolling pin or meat mallet and place in a pan with the chicken stock, chicken, curry paste and shallot; bring to the boil.

**2** Add the mushrooms to the pan and simmer gently for 8–10 minutes.

**3** Stir the sugar and fish sauce into the soup and simmer for 3 minutes until the chicken is cooked. Squeeze in the lemon juice and season to taste.

**4** Ladle the soup into bowls and scatter over the salad onion, chilli and coriander. Serve immediately.

**TRY THIS:** If any of my family are feeling a bit off colour, I throw lots of shredded root ginger into the broth for a really soothing soup – especially good for coughs and colds.

# Curried mussel soup

No, really, try it – it's fantastic, especially with the Green Onion Chapatis (page 117) or Tabletop Naan with Spicy Fried Onions (page 116).

**PREPARATION: 20 minutes  COOKING TIME: 20 minutes**

## SERVES 4

pinch of saffron strands

450 ml (¾ pint) hot vegetable stock

2 kg (4½ lb) fresh, live mussels, cleaned

150 ml (¼ pint) dry white wine

knob of butter

1 shallot, finely chopped

2 garlic cloves, peeled and finely chopped

1 small hot chilli, seeded and finely chopped

2 cm (¾ inch) piece fresh root ginger, finely chopped

½ teaspoon ground turmeric

½ teaspoon garam masala

150 ml carton double cream

juice of ½ lime

salt and freshly ground black pepper

1 tablespoon chopped fresh dill

## METHOD

**1** Place the saffron in a heatproof bowl and pour over the hot stock; set aside to infuse.

**2** Place the mussels in a large pan and pour over the wine. Cover with a tight-fitting lid and cook for 5 minutes or so, shaking the pan occasionally until the shells open.

**3** Strain the mussel liquid into a clean bowl.

**4** Heat the butter in a large pan and gently cook the shallot, garlic, chilli and ginger until softened and golden. Add the spices, saffron stock and mussel liquid and simmer gently for 10 minutes.

**5** Shell the mussels, saving about 20 to garnish and discarding any that don't open.

**6** Stir the mussels and cream into the pan, add a squeeze of lime juice and season to taste. Warm through gently, stir in the dill, then ladle into bowls.

**7** Divide the reserved mussels between the bowls and serve.

# Rapido French
# onion soup and cheese croûtes

Simple but stylish, this version of the French classic is just right for a light lunch and takes minutes to make.

**PREPARATION: 15 minutes  COOKING TIME: 40 minutes**

## SERVES 2

50 g (2 oz) butter

3 large Spanish onions, sliced

1 tablespoon caster sugar

2 garlic cloves, crushed

150 ml (¼ pint) dry white wine

600 ml (1 pint) hot, fresh chicken or vegetable stock

1 tablespoon Worcestershire sauce

1 small baguette

100 g (4 oz) Gruyère, finely grated

1 tablespoon French brandy (optional but dee-lish)

salt and freshly ground black pepper

## METHOD

**1** Melt the butter in a large pan and add the sliced onions. Sprinkle in the sugar and cook over a high heat for 10–15 minutes, stirring frequently until you get a lovely caramel brown tinge to your onions. Add the garlic and cook for a further 30 seconds.

**2** Pour the wine into the pan and cook vigorously for 1–2 minutes. Stir in the hot stock and Worcestershire sauce, bring to the boil, reduce the heat and simmer for 15–20 minutes until the onions are tender.

**3** Pre-heat the grill to high. Cut four diagonal slices of baguette and toast for 1–2 minutes on each side. Reduce the grill heat to medium.

**4** Pile the cheese on top of the toasts. Return to the grill and cook until bubbling and golden.

**5** If using the brandy, stir it into the soup, and season to taste. Then, using a slotted spoon, divide the onions between two soup bowls. Place the cheese croûtes on top of the onions, then ladle over the hot soup.

**TRY THIS:** There are lots of different ways to avoid your eyes watering when chopping onions, for example, wearing glasses, chewing parsley or chilling your onions before slicing them.

# Succulent seafood
## and roasted vegetable soup

This is a delicious, piquant soup full of flavour and packed with tender pieces of seafood. You'll need to use the oven as well as the hob, but the end result is well worth the effort. It's a great supper when paired with chunks of crusty bread.

**PREPARATION: 15 minutes  COOKING TIME: 50 minutes**

## SERVES 6

2 red peppers, seeded and quartered

1 aubergine, quartered

4 tablespoons olive oil

sea salt and freshly ground black pepper

1 large onion, chopped

2 celery stalks, chopped

4 garlic cloves, finely chopped

½ teaspoon chilli powder

50 g (2 oz) plain flour

1.2 litres (2 pints) hot fish stock

300 ml (½ pint) creamed tomatoes or passata

2 sprigs fresh thyme

1 teaspoon caster sugar

250 g (9 oz) fillet haddock or cod, cut into 2.5 cm (1 inch) chunks

250 g (9 oz) raw tiger prawns

250 g (9 oz) squid rings

juice of 1 lime

2 tablespoons chopped fresh parsley

## METHOD

**1** Pre-heat the oven to 200°C/400°F/Gas 6. Place the peppers and aubergine in a roasting tin. Drizzle over half the olive oil, season and roast for 25 minutes until tender and a little charred.

**2** Heat the remaining oil in a large pan and cook the onion, celery and garlic for about 5 minutes. Add the chilli and flour and cook for 1 minute, stirring constantly. Gradually add the stock, then the tomatoes.

**3** Cut the peppers and aubergine into 2.5 cm (1 inch) chunks and add to the pan with the thyme and sugar. Bring to the boil, cover and simmer for 15 minutes.

**4** Add the seafood to the pan and simmer for a further 4–5 minutes until tender. Add lime juice, salt and pepper to taste. Stir in the parsley, ladle into bowls and serve with crusty bread and chilled white wine.

# Spinach, mint
## and garlic soup

It may be simple, but this soup is really bursting with fresh flavour. I like to top it with crunchy pieces of fried bacon, but leave them out and you've got a vegetarian-friendly bowlful.

**PREPARATION: 15 minutes  COOKING TIME: 30 minutes**

## SERVES 4

2 tablespoons olive oil

2 large white onions, roughly chopped

2 garlic cloves, roughly chopped

1 red chilli, finely chopped

1 bunch fresh mint, roughly chopped

1 bunch fresh parsley or coriander, roughly chopped

1.2 litres (2 pints) hot vegetable stock

75 g (3 oz) cubed pancetta or lardons

500 g (1 lb 2 oz) fresh young spinach, roughly chopped

juice of 1–2 lemons

salt and freshly ground black pepper

## METHOD

1  Heat the oil in a large pan and cook the onions, garlic and chilli for 10 minutes until softened and golden. Add the herbs and stock, bring to the boil and simmer for 15 minutes.

2  Meanwhile, cook the bacon in a non-stick frying-pan until crisp and nicely browned. Drain on kitchen paper.

3  Add the spinach to the onion mixture and cook for 2 minutes. Add lemon juice, and salt and pepper to taste. Using a hand-blender, whizz the soup to a coarse purée. Ladle into bowls, scatter over the crispy bacon and a good grinding of black pepper, and serve with crusty bread.

**CHEF'S TIP:** Don't make this soup too far ahead of time – although it would still taste great, its lovely bright green colour would begin to fade.

# Newfoundland
# crab chowder

If you've never made chowder, this is the perfect place to start as it's so very easy. The potato base makes it a truly hearty soup, so you could easily serve it as a casual main meal. Canned crab is a great addition to this dish, but I've also made it with cubes of smoked fish, such as haddock, or large, juicy prawns. So go on, have a go – you won't be disappointed.

**PREPARATION: 10 minutes  COOKING TIME: 35 minutes**

## SERVES 4

25 g (1 oz) butter

4 rashers smoked streaky bacon, roughly chopped

2 shallots, finely chopped

450 g (1 lb) floury potatoes, diced

2 thyme sprigs

1 bay leaf

1.2 litres (2 pints) fish stock

2 x 170 g cans crabmeat, drained

200 g carton crème fraîche

4 tablespoons chopped fresh parsley

salt and freshly ground black pepper

## METHOD

**1** Melt the butter in a large pan and cook the bacon, shallots and potatoes for 4–5 minutes. Add the thyme, bay leaf and fish stock, bring to the boil and simmer for 25–30 minutes.

**2** Stir the crabmeat and crème fraîche into the pan and heat through gently. Stir in the parsley and season to taste. Ladle into bowls and serve.

**TRY THIS:** In Newfoundland they always crumble crackers into their chowder at the table, and I find this a really good way to serve it – just scrunch them in your hand and scatter over the top of your soup immediately before you eat it.

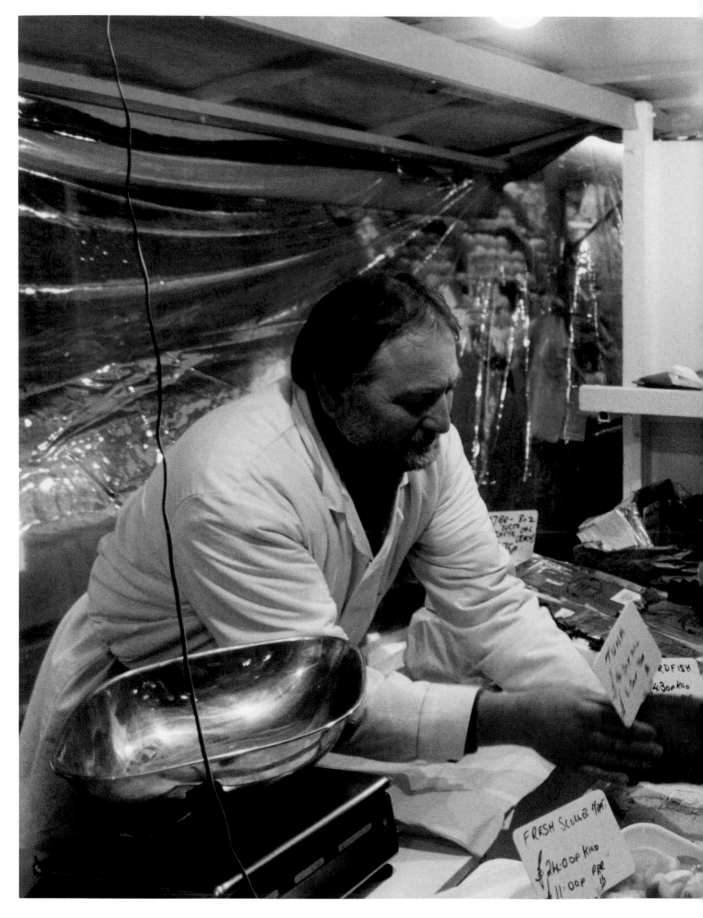

# Pacific prawn fu-yung

'Fu-yung' just means a Chinese egg dish. Here, to go with the prawns, I like to add a bit of shredded Chinese pork or sausage, or you can always throw in a bit of shredded ham if you like. Serve with a dollop of my Easy Mint Chutney (page 135) or Sweet Chilli Sauce (page 143).

**PREPARATION: 15 minutes  COOKING TIME: 10 minutes**

## SERVES 4

6 eggs

100 ml (3½ fl oz) chicken stock

2 tablespoons vegetable oil

4 salad onions, thinly sliced

1 red chilli, seeded and finely chopped

75 g (3 oz) shiitake mushrooms, thinly sliced

175 g (6 oz) cooked peeled prawns

100 g (4 oz) pork or ham, shredded

75 g (3 oz) beansprouts

1 tablespoon soy sauce

handful of fresh coriander leaves

## METHOD

**1** Beat together the eggs and stock until well blended.

**2** Heat the oil in a large frying-pan and stir-fry the salad onions, chilli and mushrooms over a medium heat until beginning to soften.

**3** Add the prawns, pork or ham and beansprouts, cook for 30 seconds, then add the soy sauce and coriander.

**4** Pour over the beaten egg mixture and cook gently, stirring, until the egg is just set; serve immediately.

# Deep-fried cod
## in beer batter

Yes, this is a proper tasty batter to coat a nice piece of cod. It's the air in the beer that gives the batter a good crunchy finish, so, unlike other batters, don't rest this one – use it as soon as it's ready. Try to choose a high-quality beer with a malty flavour for a really great batter. Deep-fry until crisp and golden, and serve with my Perfect Golden, Crispy Chips (page 111) and Minted Mushy Chip-shop Peas (page 125) or Real Tartare Sauce (page 137).

**PREPARATION: 5 minutes  COOKING TIME: 20 minutes**

## SERVES 4

4 x 175 g (6 oz) pieces of cod

salt and freshly ground black pepper

200 g (7 oz) plain flour, plus extra for dusting

½ teaspoon salt

1 egg, beaten

330 ml bottle of beer

vegetable oil, for deep-frying

lemon wedges, to garnish

## METHOD

**1** Lightly season the fish and dust with flour.

**2** Sift the flour and salt into a large bowl. Make a well in the centre, crack in the egg and gradually add the beer, stirring continuously, to make a smooth, frothy batter.

**3** Dip the fish in the batter, making sure it is well covered, and shake off any excess. Deep-fry in hot oil for 4–5 minutes until crisp and golden. Drain on kitchen paper and serve hot, garnished with the lemon wedges.

**TRY THIS.** This quantity of batter is more than enough for four pieces of fish, so why not try dipping a few extras, such as red onion rings, to serve on the side?

# Classic family fish cakes

These crisp-crumb fish cakes are a real family classic. I like to serve them with my Real Tartare Sauce (page 137) and a leafy salad such as the Rocket and Roast Onion Salad (page 120), or push the boat out and go for Perfect Golden, Crispy Chips (page 111) and Minted Mushy Chip-shop Peas (page 125).

**PREPARATION: 25 minutes  COOKING TIME: 15 minutes**

## SERVES 4

450 g (1 lb) floury potatoes, cubed

450 g (1 lb) smoked haddock

1 hard-boiled egg, chopped

2 tablespoons snipped chives or chopped fresh parsley

salt and freshly ground black pepper

2 tablespoons seasoned flour

1 egg, beaten

100 g (4 oz) white breadcrumbs

vegetable oil, for shallow-frying

## METHOD

**1**  Cook the potatoes in a pan of boiling, salted water until tender. Drain and mash well.

**2**  Meanwhile, place the fish in a sauté-pan or frying-pan and cover with boiling water. Bring to the boil and simmer for 5 minutes until just cooked.

**3**  Drain the fish and remove the skin. Using a fork, flake the fish, discarding any bones. Mix together the potatoes, fish, boiled egg, chives and salt and pepper. Use your hands to shape the mixture into 4 or 8 even-sized round or triangular cakes.

**4**  Dust the fish cakes with the seasoned flour, dip in the beaten egg, then coat in the breadcrumbs, making sure they are completely covered.

**5**  Heat the oil in a frying-pan and shallow-fry for 3–4 minutes on each side until crisp and golden. Serve warm.

Classic family fish cakes *with* Real tartare sauce

# Golden crumb-crunch scampi

Scampi is actually the tail of the langoustine, which is also known as the Dublin Bay prawn. These can be quite hard to find, and can also be quite pricey, so I often find it easier to make mine using fresh tiger prawns – though if you can get hold of the real thing, do give it a go. Because of the lovely fresh taste of the prawns, I prefer to keep this dish really simple and serve the scampi with a good dollop of my home-made Real Tartare Sauce (page 137) and a simple mixed salad made from lettuce, cucumber and tomatoes.

**PREPARATION: 10 minutes  COOKING TIME: 10 minutes**

## SERVES 4

vegetable oil, for deep-frying

32 large, raw tiger prawns, shelled

4 tablespoons seasoned flour

2 beaten eggs

75 g (3 oz) natural dried breadcrumbs

sea salt

lemon wedges and tartare sauce, to serve

## METHOD

**1** Heat about 6 cm (2½ inches) of vegetable oil in a wok or deep frying-pan.

**2** Toss the prawns first in the seasoned flour, then the beaten egg. Give them a good shake to remove excess egg, then finally toss in the breadcrumbs. Deep-fry in batches for 2–3 minutes until golden brown and cooked through. Drain on kitchen paper and serve immediately.

**TRY THIS:** It's really important to use dried breadcrumbs for this dish as the crunchy coating is a lovely contrast to the juicy interior. I find supermarket breadcrumbs work very well, but if you have any stale white sliced bread, arrange it on a tray and leave to dry out completely. Once hard and dry, whizz in a food processor to form fine crumbs, then store in an airtight jar until ready to use.

# Ocean cheese and potato pie

This is a fabulous twist on a classic family dish. It's great for after-work suppers because you can prepare the mash and the fish filling the day before. When you're ready to eat, spoon the mash over the fish mixture and pop it in the oven for 20 minutes. Sprinkle over the cheese and finish it off as described in step 5 below.

**PREPARATION: 15 minutes  COOKING TIME: 20 minutes**

## SERVES 4

1 kg (2¼ lb) floury potatoes, cubed

450 ml (¾ pint) milk

250 g (9 oz) smoked haddock

50 g (2 oz) butter

25 g (1oz) plain flour

200 g (7 oz) Cheddar, grated

4 tablespoons fromage frais

150 g (5 oz) frozen peas

200 g (7 oz) large, cooked, peeled prawns

2 tablespoons snipped chives

salt and freshly ground black pepper

## METHOD

1 Cook the potatoes in a large pan of boiling, salted water until tender.

2 Heat the milk in a frying-pan, add the haddock and poach for 5 minutes or so until just cooked. Transfer the fish to a plate and leave to cool. Do not discard the poaching milk.

3 Melt half the butter in a pan and stir in the flour. Cook gently for 1 minute, stirring continuously. Gradually add the poaching milk, stirring to make a smooth sauce. Bring to the boil, then remove from the heat and stir in three-quarters of the grated cheese, plus the fromage frais, peas, prawns and chives.

4 Flake in the fish, discarding the skin and any bones, and season to taste. Transfer to a heatproof dish.

5 Pre-heat the grill to medium. Drain the potatoes, mash well with the remaining butter and season to taste. Spoon the mash over the fish mixture and scatter the reserved cheese on top. Grind over some black pepper, then cook under the grill for 3–4 minutes until the top is golden. Serve warm.

# Prawn and peanut pan-fried udon

Udon noodles are those lovely, thick white noodles you can buy now. A lot of supermarkets stock fresh ones, which are vacuum packed, so they have a long shelf life. If you have trouble finding them, use regular Chinese-style egg noodles.

**PREPARATION: 15 minutes  COOKING TIME: 15 minutes**

## SERVES 4

300 g (11 oz) dried udon noodles or 500 g (1 lb 2 oz) fresh

vegetable oil, for frying

4 shallots, very finely sliced

2 large red chillies, seeded and thinly sliced

2 teaspoons sesame oil

300 g (11 oz) large, cooked, peeled prawns

200 g (7 oz) fresh beansprouts

handful of fresh coriander leaves

2 fresh limes, cut into wedges, for serving

### FOR THE PEANUT SAUCE

200 g (7 oz) salted roasted peanuts

2 garlic cloves, peeled

2.5 cm (1 inch) piece root ginger, peeled and roughly chopped

200 ml carton coconut cream

1 tablespoon soy sauce

1 teaspoon hot chilli sauce

## METHOD

**1** Plunge the noodles into a large pan of boiling water. Bring back to the boil, simmer for 1 minute until tender, then drain well. Cool under cold water.

**2** Make the sauce: place the peanuts, garlic and ginger in a food processor and whizz until finely chopped. Transfer to a bowl and stir in the coconut cream; add soy and chilli sauces, to taste.

**3** Heat 1 cm (½ inch) of vegetable oil in a wok or large frying-pan. When the oil is very hot, add the shallots and chillies and cook for 3–4 minutes until crisp and golden brown. Drain on kitchen paper.

**4** Pour most of the oil out of the wok, leaving just a thin coating, then add the sesame oil. Cook the noodles for 1–2 minutes, then stir in the prawns and peanut sauce; stir in enough water (200–300 ml/ 7–10 fl oz) – to make a thick, glossy sauce and cook for 3–4 minutes until piping hot.

**5** Stir in the beansprouts and coriander. Divide between plates and scatter over the crispy shallot mixture. Serve with wedges of lime for squeezing over.

# Devilled, dusted whitebait

This is a traditional pub dish – truly delicious. Serve unadorned as a starter, or make it a main course by serving it with some lovely crusty bread and a crisp green salad – you can't go wrong.

**PREPARATION: 5 minutes  COOKING TIME: 5 minutes**

## SERVES 4

375 g (13 oz) whitebait, thawed if frozen

25 g (1 oz) plain flour

½ teaspoon salt

1 teaspoon English mustard powder

½ teaspoon cayenne pepper, plus extra for dusting

½ teaspoon paprika

finely grated rind of 1 lemon

vegetable oil, for deep-frying

lemon wedges and herb sprigs, to serve

## METHOD

1  Rinse the whitebait and pat dry with kitchen paper.

2  Place the flour, salt, mustard, cayenne, paprika and lemon rind in a polythene bag. Add the whitebait and shake well to coat.

3  Deep-fry the whitebait in hot oil for 2 minutes until golden. Drain on kitchen paper. Transfer to a serving platter and dust with a little cayenne. Garnish with lemon wedges and herb sprigs and serve immediately.

# Classic moules marinière

This French classic is really easy to make, and when mussels are in season – September to April – they're cheap and plentiful. Serve with salad, crusty bread and a glass of your favourite chilled white wine – ooh la la!

**PREPARATION: 10 minutes  COOKING TIME: 15 minutes**

## SERVES 4

25 g (1 oz) butter

1 onion, chopped

2 garlic cloves, finely chopped

150 ml (¼ pint) dry white wine

150 ml (¼ pint) fish stock

2 kg (4½ lb) live, clean mussels

3 tablespoons double cream

2 tablespoons chopped fresh parsley

salt and freshly ground black pepper

## METHOD

**1** Melt the butter in a large pan and cook the onion and garlic for 3–4 minutes until softened and golden. Then pour in the wine, bring to the boil and add the mussels.

**2** Cover and cook over a high heat for 4–5 minutes until all the shells have opened. Transfer the mussels to a serving dish, discarding any that remain closed, leaving the juices behind.

**3** Add the fish stock to the juices, bring to the boil, then reduce the heat. Stir the cream and parsley into the pan juices, add pepper and check for salt. Ladle the pan juices over the mussels and serve hot.

# Roasted
# lemon bay garlic cod

This is a really light dish – I've simply marinated the fish with a little garlic and parsley, and cooked it over bay and lemon so it picks up the fragrance. Serve with a leafy salad or my New Millennium Posh Potato Salad (page 129) or Mozzamary Garlic Bread (page 118) and a good bottle of Chardonnay for a lovely lunch.

**PREPARATION: 10 minutes + 10 minutes marinating  COOKING TIME: 10 minutes**

## SERVES 4

4 garlic cloves, crushed

1 tablespoon chopped fresh parsley

2 tablespoons olive oil

salt and freshly ground black pepper

4 x 150 g (5 oz) cod fillets

2 lemons, thinly sliced

10 fresh bay leaves

## METHOD

**1** Preheat the oven to 220°C/425°F/Gas 7. Mix together the garlic, parsley, olive oil and some salt and pepper. Rub the mixture over the fish fillets and set aside for 10 minutes or so.

**2** Arrange the lemons and bay leaves on a baking sheet and sit the cod fillets on top. Cook in the hot oven for 8–10 minutes until just cooked and a little charred. Serve immediately.

Roasted lemon bay garlic cod *with* Warm sweet potato and roast tomato cheese salad

# Lobster
## and papaya salad

Here's a touch of luxury when you're feeling a bit flash. Ask the fishmonger to halve the lobster and remove all the meat for you – alternatively, you can buy lobster ready prepared in supermarkets. Serve with warm baby new potatoes in their skins for an exquisite main course, or how about my New Millennium Posh Potato Salad (page 129)?

**PREPARATION: 10 minutes**

## SERVES 2

1 kg (2¼ lb) lobster, cooked and shelled

60 g bag baby salad leaves

1 papaya, skinned, seeded and sliced

1 avocado, skinned, stoned and sliced

1 tablespoon raspberry vinegar

2 tablespoons olive oil

salt and freshly ground black pepper

chervil or dill sprigs, to garnish

## METHOD

**1** Cut the lobster meat into 2 cm (¾ inch) slices or chunks.

**2** Divide the salad leaves between 2 large plates and arrange the papaya and avocado slices on top of the leaves. Add the lobster meat.

**3** Whisk together the vinegar, olive oil and some salt and pepper, then drizzle over the salad.

**4** Garnish with herb sprigs and serve.

# Crispy cache calamari

Memories of Mediterranean holidays come flooding back, as there's nothing like a plateful of crispy calamari and a glass of dry white wine to make you enjoy the summer – also fantastic for a weekend lunch in the garden. I use a very simple egg-free batter for a really crisp result that's heavenly to eat. I only wish the sun would shine! I like to serve it tapas style, with Jacqueline's Potato Skins with Guacamole (page 106), a fresh tomato salad and some juicy black olives.

**PREPARATION: 10 minutes  COOKING TIME: 10 minutes**

## SERVES 4

175 g (6 oz) self-raising flour

1 teaspoon paprika, plus extra for dusting

½ teaspoon salt

450 g (1 lb) cleaned fresh squid cut into 1 cm (½ inch) wide rings

4 tablespoons seasoned flour, for dusting

vegetable oil, for deep-frying

cayenne pepper (optional) and lemon and lime wedges, to garnish

## METHOD

1 Sift the flour, paprika and salt into a bowl. Gradually beat in 250 ml (8 fl oz) water to make a smooth batter.

2 Dust the squid in the seasoned flour, then dip in the batter, shaking off any excess. Deep-fry for about 3–4 minutes until crisp and golden. Drain on kitchen paper.

3 Transfer the calamari to serving plates, dust with paprika or cayenne pepper, garnish with lemon and lime wedges and serve.

**TRY THIS:** The tentacles are just as tasty as the body of the squid. Make sure the 'beak' has been removed (check with your fishmonger: If you can't, it's the hard, crusty bit directly above the tentacles), then batter and fry as for the rings above.

# Tuna burgers
## with red onion salsa

A great recipe for meaty fish, such as tuna. I've added wasabi, which is Japanese horseradish, and it gives a fantastic kick to the fish, though you can add a dab of English mustard if you can't get hold of it. This stylish dish is a perfect starter for a dinner party, but makes a terrific main course supper if served with Grate Hash Browns (page 113) or chips (page 111).

**PREPARATION: 25 minutes  COOKING TIME: 10 minutes**

## SERVES 4

### FOR THE SALSA

1 red onion, finely diced

2 plum tomatoes, seeded and finely chopped

1 green chilli, seeded and finely chopped

juice of 1 lime

1 tablespoon olive oil

salt and freshly ground black pepper

### FOR THE BURGERS

400 g (14 oz) fresh tuna

1–2 teaspoons wasabi paste

1 tablespoon sesame seeds

salt and freshly ground black pepper

1 tablespoon seasoned flour

vegetable oil, for shallow-frying

1 ciabatta loaf, sliced and toasted

## METHOD

**1** Begin by making the salsa: stir all the ingredients together, and set aside at room temperature for at least an hour.

**2** Place the tuna in a food processor and pulse until coarsely minced. Mix with the wasabi paste, sesame seeds and some salt and pepper. With damp hands, shape the mixture into 4 even-sized burgers.

**3** Dust the burgers in the seasoned flour, shaking off any excess. Shallow-fry for 2–4 minutes on each side until golden brown and just cooked through. Be careful not to overcook them or they'll quickly become dry.

**4** Place the tuna burgers on the toasted ciabatta and top with a dollop of the salsa. Garnish with slices of fresh lime and serve warm.

# Peppy's barbecue chicken
## with Jamaican fried dumplings

The herby fried dumplings are the perfect accompaniment to my mum's spicy barbecue chicken. For an extra kick, why not add a ¼ teaspoon of chilli flakes to the dumpling mixture and wash it down with a glass of my Sweet 'n' Easy Mango Lassi (page 166).

**PREPARATION: 15 minutes + 20 minutes marinating  COOKING TIME: 15 minutes**

## SERVES 4

4 tablespoons tomato ketchup

juice of 1 large lemon

2 tablespoons soy sauce

1 tablespoon dark brown sugar

½ teaspoon ground allspice (Jamaican pepper)

½ teaspoon cayenne pepper

½ teaspoon salt

4 skinless, boneless chicken breasts

### FOR THE FRIED DUMPLINGS

200 g (7 oz) plain flour

1 teaspoon baking powder

2 tablespoons finely chopped parsley

½ teaspoon dried thyme

½ teaspoon salt

200 ml (7 fl oz) milk

vegetable oil, for deep-frying

## METHOD

**1** In a large bowl, mix together the ketchup, lemon juice, soy sauce, sugar, allspice, cayenne and salt. Add the chicken breasts, stirring to coat in the marinade, then cover and set aside for 20 minutes or so.

**2** Meanwhile, make the dumplings: mix together the flour, baking powder, herbs and salt. Beat in the milk to make a thick batter.

**3** Heat 5 cm (2 inches) of oil in a wok or deep frying-pan – the oil should be hot enough so that when a cube of bread is added to the pan, it browns in about 1½ minutes. Cook spoonfuls of the mixture, in batches, for 3–4 minutes until puffed, golden brown and cooked through. Drain on kitchen paper.

**4** Cook the chicken on a hot barbecue or in an oiled griddle pan for 8–10 minutes on each side until well browned and cooked through. Serve with mixed salad leaves drizzled with olive oil and lemon juice.

# Charred chicken and pepper fajitas

The sight and sound of sizzling chicken and crispy vegetables arriving at your table is a joy to behold, and it doesn't have to be in a restaurant: this can be achieved at home for a fraction of the cost.

**PREPARATION: 15 minutes  COOKING TIME: 10 minutes**

## SERVES 2

2 large skinless, boneless chicken breasts, cut into 1 cm (½ inch) wide strips

1 yellow pepper, cut lengthways into 1 cm (½ inch) wide strips

1 red onion, thickly sliced

½ teaspoon dried oregano

¼ teaspoon crushed chillies

2 tablespoons vegetable oil

grated rind and juice of 1 lime

salt and freshly ground black pepper

4 x 20 cm (8 inch) flour tortillas

sunflower oil, for brushing

leafy salad, to serve

150 ml carton soured cream

## METHOD

**1** Place the chicken strips, pepper, red onion, oregano, chillies, oil, lime rind and juice in a large bowl. Add plenty of seasoning and toss together until well mixed.

**2** Heat a flat griddle or heavy non-stick frying-pan. Add the chicken mixture and cook over a high heat for 6–8 minutes, turning once or twice, until the mixture is well browned, lightly charred and cooked through.

**3** Brush the tortillas with sunflower oil and briefly warm them in the microwave for 10 seconds, or heat them in a dry frying-pan for a few seconds on each side.

**4** Serve separately, or pile the fajitas in the middle of your warm tortillas, add salad and a dollop of soured cream, roll up and enjoy. Serve with a bottle or two of chilled Mexican lager – *salud*!

# Cheeky chicken tikka masala

Forget having to wait for your take-away chicken tikka: this is one of the easiest curries there is to make. If it's summer, why not have a go at cooking the chicken skewers over the old barbie?

**PREPARATION: 20 minutes + 2 hours marinating   COOKING TIME: 25 minutes**

## SERVES 4

4 skinless, boneless chicken breasts, cubed

2.5 cm (1 inch) piece root ginger, finely chopped

2 garlic cloves, finely chopped

1 teaspoon chilli powder

salt and freshly ground black pepper

2 tablespoons chopped fresh coriander

juice of 1 lime

2 tablespoons vegetable oil

1 onion, finely chopped

1 red chilli, seeded and finely chopped

1 teaspoon ground turmeric

300 ml carton double cream

juice of ½ lemon

Pulao Rice (page 122) or Tabletop Naan with Spicy Fried Onions (page 116), to serve

handful of fresh coriander leaves, to garnish

## METHOD

**1** Place the chicken breasts in a large bowl and mix with the ginger, garlic, chilli, salt, pepper, coriander, lime juice and 1 tablespoon of the oil. Set aside for 2 hours.

**2** Pre-heat the grill to high. Thread the chicken on to skewers and cook under the grill for 12 minutes or so, turning frequently until well browned.

**3** Meanwhile, heat the remaining oil in a large pan and cook the onion and chilli for 5–8 minutes until dark golden. Add the turmeric and cook for 30 seconds. Stir in the cream and cook gently for a couple of minutes.

**4** Slide the chicken off the skewers and stir into the creamy sauce. Simmer for 5 minutes or so until the chicken is cooked through. Check the seasoning, adding some lemon juice to taste, and serve with rice or naan. Garnish with the coriander.

# Wok-it chicken chow mein

If you've got some roast chicken left over from last night's dinner, simply shred it up and make this lovely chicken chow mein – perfect for a quick supper. One of those packets of fresh stir-fry vegetables is great to have on stand-by for this.

**PREPARATION: 10 minutes  COOKING TIME: 15 minutes**

## SERVES 2

175 g (6 oz) egg noodles

1 tablespoon sunflower oil

1 onion, thinly sliced

2 garlic cloves, thinly sliced

1 cm (½ inch) piece root ginger, finely chopped (optional)

100 g (4 oz) beansprouts

100 g (4 oz) mangetout, halved lengthways, or peas

175 g (6 oz) cooked chicken, shredded

1 tablespoon soy sauce

1 tablespoon Sweet Chilli Sauce (page 143)

## METHOD

**1** Cook the noodles in a large pan of boiling, salted water according to the packet instructions.

**2** Meanwhile, heat the oil in a wok and stir-fry the onion over a high heat for 2–3 minutes until beginning to brown. Add the garlic, ginger (if using), beansprouts and mangetout or peas and stir-fry for 1 minute.

**3** Drain the noodles well and add to the wok with the chicken and soy sauce; cook for 2 minutes until piping hot. Stir in the sweet chilli sauce and serve immediately.

# Scrunchy
# sweet and sour chicken

Chicken and pineapple is a wonderful combination, and this dish shows it off to great effect. It has a lovely fresh flavour that's sure to be popular with all the family. I like to serve it with Excellent Egg and Ginger Fried Rice (page 110).

**PREPARATION: 20 minutes  COOKING TIME: 15 minutes**

## SERVES 4

2 egg yolks

2 tablespoons cornflour

salt and freshly ground black pepper

4 skinless, boneless chicken breasts, cubed

vegetable oil, for deep-frying

**FOR THE SWEET AND SOUR SAUCE**

1 onion, sliced

1 small red pepper, cut into 2.5 cm (1 inch) pieces

1 small orange pepper, cut into 2.5 cm (1 inch) pieces

435 g can pineapple cubes in natural juice

1 tablespoon cornflour

2 tablespoons tomato ketchup

2 tablespoons light soy sauce

1 tablespoon white wine vinegar

handful of fresh coriander leaves, to garnish

## METHOD

**1** Mix together the egg yolks with a tablespoon of water, the cornflour and some salt and pepper.

**2** Heat 5 cm (2 inches) of oil in a wok or deep frying-pan. Toss the chicken in the cornflour mixture and deep-fry in batches for 5 minutes or so until crisp and golden. Drain on kitchen paper.

**3** Empty the oil from the wok to leave a thin coating in the pan. Stir-fry the onion and peppers over a high heat for 2–3 minutes. Strain the pineapple cubes (reserving the juice), add to the pan and cook for a minute or two.

**4** Mix together the cornflour and a little of the pineapple juice to form a paste, then stir in the remaining juice, the ketchup, soy sauce, vinegar and 135 ml (4½ fl oz) water. Pour this into the pan and bring to the boil, stirring until the mixture thickens.

**5** Stir the chicken pieces into the pan and simmer for 5 minutes until cooked through. Check the seasoning, then divide between bowls, scatter over the coriander and serve.

Scrunchy sweet and sour chicken *with* Excellent egg and ginger fried rice

# Sticky maple syrup ribs

I love a sticky rib, and there's loads of different ways to marinate or glaze them. This is an easy and tasty way to get good results, and works well on the barbie too. Go easy on the chilli flakes if the kids are joining in. Try serving the ribs with Buttered Slam Jackets (page 102) and a side order of Citrus Couscous and Sultana Salad (page 130).

**PREPARATION: 10 minutes  COOKING TIME: 40 minutes**

## SERVES 4

2 tablespoons tomato purée

1 tablespoon cornflour

juice of 2 limes

2 tablespoons maple syrup

2 garlic cloves, crushed

½ teaspoon dried chilli flakes

½ teaspoon salt

750 g (1½ lb) pork ribs

## METHOD

**1** Mix together the tomato purée and cornflour to make a paste. Stir in the lime juice, maple syrup, garlic, chilli and salt.

**2** Pre-heat the grill to medium. Rub the mixture into the pork ribs then arrange on a grill rack. Cook under the grill or on a barbecue for 30 minutes, turning occasionally, until well cooked and nicely browned. You can also cook them in the oven if you prefer: pre-heat the oven to 190°C/375°F/Gas 5, pop the ribs on a wire rack, place on a baking tray and cook for 35–45 minutes.

**TRY THIS:** This glaze is also very tasty on other cuts of pork, such as steaks or chops, but you will need to reduce the cooking time if the meat is boneless.

# Crisp-crumbed
# pan pork escalopes

This is a favourite dish in my house as it's lovely straight from the pan– especially when accompanied by some lovely Breaking Bubble and Savoy Squeak (page 107) and grilled tomatoes. Any left-overs are great the next day, sandwiched between a couple of slices of crusty white bread and topped with a squirt of mayonnaise or a dash of brown sauce – salivating!

**PREPARATION: 20 minutes  COOKING TIME: 15 minutes**

## SERVES 4

500 g (1 lb 2 oz) pork fillet or boneless loin chops

2 garlic cloves, crushed

1 tablespoon Dijon mustard

¼ teaspoon cayenne pepper or chilli powder

salt and freshly ground black pepper

100 g (4 oz) fresh white breadcrumbs

2 tablespoons freshly grated Parmesan

2 tablespoons seasoned flour

2 eggs, beaten

vegetable oil, for shallow-frying

lemon wedges, to serve

## METHOD

**1** If using pork fillet, cut into 2 cm (¾ inch) slices. Place a piece of sliced pork or a chop on a sheet of greaseproof paper or plastic wrap, cover with a second sheet and, using a rolling pin or meat mallet, flatten to a thickness of about 5 mm (¼ inch). Repeat for the remaining meat (or ask your butcher to do this for you).

**2** Mix together the garlic, mustard, cayenne or chilli powder and a little salt and pepper and spread over the pork. Stir together the breadcrumbs and Parmesan.

**3** Toss the pork in the seasoned flour, shaking off any excess, dip in the beaten egg and then into the cheesy breadcrumbs, to coat.

**4** Heat the oil in a large frying-pan and shallow-fry in batches for 3 minutes on each side until golden brown and cooked through. Drain on kitchen paper and serve warm.

**TRY THIS:** This method also works very well with frying steak, chicken and turkey breasts.

# Thai-style
## yellow pork curry

If you like creamy, delicate curries, this is the one for you. To enhance the flavour, serve with plain boiled jasmine rice and a side order of Tabletop Naan (page 116) to help mop up all those lovely coconutty juices.

**PREPARATION: 15 minutes  COOKING TIME: 20 minutes**

## SERVES 4

2 tablespoons vegetable oil

2 salad onions, thinly sliced

1 garlic clove, thinly sliced

500 g (1 lb 2 oz) pork fillet, cubed

1 aubergine, cubed

400 ml can coconut milk

3 kaffir lime leaves, shredded

2 teaspoons yellow or green Thai curry paste

150 g (5 oz) shiitake mushrooms, sliced

220 g can sliced water chestnuts, drained

2 tablespoons light soy sauce

1 teaspoon fish sauce

handful fresh basil leaves

2 limes, cut into wedges

## METHOD

**1**  Heat the oil in a large pan and cook the salad onions and garlic for 2 minutes. Add the pork and aubergine and stir-fry for 3–4 minutes until the pork turns creamy white.

**2**  Stir in the coconut milk, lime leaves and curry paste and simmer for 10 minutes.

**3**  Add the shiitake mushrooms and water chestnuts and cook for a further 5 minutes. Stir in the soy sauce, fish sauce and fresh basil leaves. Serve with plain rice and lime wedges for squeezing over.

# Gina's classic super shepherd's pie

You've seen it before, but you really can't beat an old classic, and this is one of my family's favourites. What's different is the addition of soy sauce and Tabasco for a real kick and guaranteed clean bowls. My neighbour Gina thinks it's *suuper*!

**PREPARATION: 10 minutes  COOKING TIME: 25 minutes**

## SERVES 2

450 g (1 lb) floury potatoes, diced

1 tablespoon vegetable oil

1 large carrot, diced

1 small onion, finely chopped

300 g (11 oz) minced lamb

300 ml (½ pint) hot lamb stock

1 tablespoon brown sauce

2 teaspoons soy sauce

2 tablespoons milk

knob of butter

1 teaspoon cornflour

75 g (3 oz) frozen peas

salt and freshly ground black pepper

few drops of Tabasco

100 g (4 oz) grated Cheddar – optional but nice

## METHOD

**1**  Cook the potatoes in a large pan of boiling, salted water for 10–12 minutes until tender.

**2**  Meanwhile, heat the oil in a large frying-pan and cook the carrot and onion for about 1 minute over a medium–high heat, then add the lamb mince and stir-fry until well browned. Pour in the hot stock and stir in the brown sauce and soy sauce. Bring to the boil and simmer rapidly for 3–4 minutes.

**3**  Drain the potatoes well and return to the pan, mash well, then beat in the milk and butter until smooth and creamy.

**4**  Mix the cornflour and a little water to a paste, and stir into the lamb mixture with the peas; bring back to the boil, stirring, until slightly thickened. Season with salt, pepper and Tabasco, to taste.

**5**  Pre-heat the grill to medium. Spoon the mince mixture into a heatproof dish and top with the mashed potato. Using a fork, mark a criss-cross pattern on the top and sprinkle over the grated cheese. Place under the grill for 3 minutes until the pie is speckled with brown or lovely and golden if using cheese.

# Granny's corned-beef hash and fried egg

This is wonderful comfort food that I first tasted when it was cooked by the granny of one of my mates. Obviously, garlic and Tabasco have been added by me for one reason – *taste*. No wonder we covered the original in ketchup – sorry, Gran. Serve with greens or bok choi stir-fried in sesame oil, a splash of soy sauce and a teaspoon of runny honey – yummy!

**PREPARATION: 10 minutes  COOKING TIME: 25 minutes**

## SERVES 2

350 g (12 oz) floury potatoes, peeled and diced

1–2 tablespoons vegetable oil

1 small onion, chopped

2 garlic cloves, crushed

200 g can corned beef

few shakes of Tabasco or other chilli sauce

2 eggs

knob of butter

salt and freshly ground black pepper

## METHOD

**1** Cook the potatoes in a large pan of boiling, salted water for 10–12 minutes until tender.

**2** Meanwhile, heat the oil in a small frying-pan and cook the onion and garlic for about 5 minutes until softened.

**3** Open the can of corned beef and turn out onto a chopping board. Chop roughly and add to the pan.

**4** Drain the potatoes well and add to the corned beef mixture. Crush with a fork, stirring to combine the mixture. Cook for 5 minutes until a crust forms on the bottom. Add salt, pepper and a shake of Tabasco then break up the mixture.

**5** Add more oil if necessary and continue to cook the mixture until the base is golden and crusty. Break up once more and leave to cook again until crusty underneath.

**6** Meanwhile, heat a small frying-pan, add the knob of butter. When it's beginning to melt and foam break in the eggs and cook, preferably sunny side up. Divide the hash between two plates, slide an egg on top of each and serve with a glass of iced lemon barley water.

# Lightning lamb dhansak

One of the most popular dishes on any Indian menu and absolutely delicious. For complete authenticity, it can take a whole day to make lamb dhansak, but this lightning version combines all the flavours and tastes superb. Tamarind paste is available in large supermarkets or good delis.

**PREPARATION: 20 minutes  COOKING TIME: 25 minutes**

## SERVES 4

500 g (1lb 2 oz) cubed lamb

2 tablespoons garam masala

2–3 tablespoons vegetable oil

2 onions, thinly sliced

2 garlic cloves, thinly sliced

200 g (7 oz) diced pumpkin or squash

100 g (4 oz) red lentils

600 ml (1 pint) hot vegetable stock

1 tablespoon curry paste

1 tablespoon tamarind paste

25 g (1 oz) caster sugar

salt and freshly ground black pepper

2 tablespoons chopped fresh mint or coriander

juice of 1 lemon

Pulao Rice (page 122), to serve

## METHOD

**1** Toss the lamb in the garam masala. Heat 1 tablespoon of the oil in a large pan and quickly brown the lamb. Transfer to a plate and set aside.

**2** Add a little more oil to the pan, then cook the onions, garlic and pumpkin or squash for 5 minutes until softened and beginning to brown.

**3** Now add the lentils, stock, curry paste, tamarind paste and sugar and return the lamb to the pan. Bring to the boil, cover and simmer for 25–30 minutes, stirring occasionally, until the mixture is thickened and the ingredients are lovely and tender.

**4** Check the seasoning, then stir in the mint or coriander and lemon juice, to taste. Serve with pulao rice.

**TRY THIS:** Use the remaining squash (or pumpkin) to make the Butternut Squash Spiced Soup on page 44.

Lightning lamb dhansak *with* Pulao rice

# Café chilli beef tacos

This is a fantastic chilli with a really developed flavour, which it gets from my secret ingredient – coffee! Try it, it really packs a punch. By serving with Buttered Slam Jackets (page 102), you'll have a fast main meal to die for.

**PREPARATION: 10 minutes  COOKING TIME: 30 minutes**

## SERVES 4

1 tablespoon vegetable oil

1 onion, finely chopped

2 garlic cloves, finely chopped

2 red chillies, seeded and finely chopped

500 g (1 lb 2 oz) minced beef

1 teaspoon Chinese five-spice powder

400 g can kidney beans, drained

400 g can chopped tomatoes

150 ml (¼ pint) strong black coffee

salt and freshly ground black pepper

8 taco shells

shredded lettuce plus soured cream and paprika, to serve

## METHOD

**1** Heat the oil in a large pan and cook the onion, garlic and chillies for 3–4 minutes until beginning to soften. Add the mince and five-spice powder and cook for a further 3–4 minutes, stirring, until the meat begins to brown.

**2** Add the kidney beans, tomatoes and coffee. Bring to the boil and simmer for 20 minutes until the mixture is thick and fairly dark. Season to taste.

**3** Fill the taco shells with shredded lettuce, then pile in the chilli mixture. Top with a spoonful of soured cream and a shake of paprika and serve. A glass of chilled Mexican lager is always a winner with this recipe.

# Pappardelle
## with chilli caper oil and baby mozzarella

For a light, versatile and fun meal this is a real winner. The combination of wonderful strong flavours with the delicate taste and texture of mozzarella blends beautifully. Great as a starter for those impromptu suppers, or simply increase the quantities and serve as a main course. Strips of Parma ham draped on top would be a lovely addition.

**PREPARATION: 15 minutes  COOKING TIME: 10 minutes**

## SERVES 4

250 g (9 oz) pasta ribbons, such as pappardelle, fettucine or lasagnette

3 tablespoons olive oil

large handful fresh basil leaves

2 garlic cloves, thinly sliced

1 red chilli, thinly sliced

2 tablespoons pickled capers, well rinsed and dried

juice of 1 lime

sea salt and freshly ground black pepper

150 g (15 oz) bocconcini (baby mozzarella), halved, or ball mozzarella, diced

## METHOD

**1** Cook the pasta in a large pan of boiling, salted water according to the packet instructions.

**2** Two minutes before the pasta is ready, heat the oil in a frying-pan and cook the basil, garlic, chilli and capers for 2 minutes. Squeeze in the lime juice and check the seasoning.

**3** Drain the pasta well and return to the pan. Toss with the infused oil mixture and the mozzarella. Divide between 4 bowls and serve with a good grinding of black pepper.

# Deep-pan American-style cheese-ring pizza crust

This is one of those thick pizzas that has the cheese inside the ring crust. It's a little more complicated than other pizzas, so if you don't want to bother making a cheese ring, simply scatter the cheese over the top.

**PREPARATION: 25 minutes + 1 hour resting  COOKING TIME: 20 minutes**

## SERVES 4

350 g (12 oz) strong white flour

1 teaspoon table salt

7 g sachet easy blend yeast

2 tablespoons olive oil

250 ml (8 fl oz) warm water

### FOR THE TOPPING AND CRUST

150 g ball mozzarella, drained

2 tablespoons chopped fresh parsley

1 garlic clove, crushed

salt and freshly ground black pepper

100 ml (3½ fl oz) passata

2 tomatoes, thinly sliced

75 g (3 oz) thinly sliced pepperoni

4 green pickled chillies, sliced

## METHOD

**1** Place the flour, salt and yeast in a food processor fitted with a dough hook. With the motor running, pour in the oil and warm water and mix to form a soft, stretchy dough. Alternatively, make the dough by hand and knead on a floured board for 5 minutes.

**2** Transfer the dough to a bowl, rub the surface with a little oil and cover with a clean, damp tea towel. Set aside at room temperature for an hour or so until the dough has roughly doubled in size. Meanwhile, roughly chop the mozzarella and mix with the parsley, garlic and some seasoning.

**3** Pre-heat the oven to 230°C/450°F/Gas 8. On a floured surface, roll the dough into a thin 40 cm (16 inch) circle. Arrange the cheese around the edge of the dough, leaving a 4 cm (1½ inch) border. Dampen the inner edge of the cheese ring, then pull the outer edge over to cover the cheese. Press down firmly to seal.

**4** Carefully turn the pizza on to a large baking sheet so the joins are underneath. Spoon the passata within the border, then scatter over the toppings. Bake for 12–15 minutes until browned and crisp. Cut into wedges and serve immediately with a lovely crisp, green salad sprinkled with olive oil and balsamic vinegar.

# Prawn and Parma pizzinis

These delightful pizzinis are a great brunch treat, or are ideal as a light snack or starter. You could also serve them with Grate Hash Browns (page 113) for a tasty family dinner – the kids love 'em too.

**PREPARATION: 15 minutes  COOKING TIME: 35 minutes**

## SERVES 4

150 g pack pizza-base mix

1 tablespoon olive oil

flour, for kneading

### FOR THE TOMATO SAUCE

250 g (9 oz) ripe tomatoes, seeded and roughly chopped

2 garlic cloves, finely chopped

4 thyme sprigs

1 tablespoon tomato purée

1 tablespoon olive oil

salt and freshly ground black pepper

### FOR THE TOPPING

200 g (7 oz) large cooked peeled prawns

4 slices Parma ham, halved lengthways

handful of fresh basil leaves

fresh Parmesan, to serve

## METHOD

**1**  Pre-heat the oven to 220°C/425°F/Gas 7. Place the pizza-base mix in a large bowl and stir in the olive oil and enough warm water (about 120 ml/4 fl oz) to make a soft dough. Knead vigorously on a lightly floured surface for about 5 minutes until smooth and elastic.

**2**  Break the dough into 4 even pieces, then pat out between the hands to make rough 12 cm (4½ inch) circles. Transfer to a large baking sheet and set aside in a warm place for 10 minutes or so to rise.

**3**  Make the tomato sauce: place the tomatoes, garlic, thyme, tomato purée and olive oil in a small pan. Simmer over a medium to high heat for 10–20 minutes, stirring occasionally until thickened and pulpy. Season to taste.

**4**  Spoon the sauce on to the dough circles, then scatter over the prawns. Ripple the strips of Parma ham across the top, then bake for 10 minutes until the pizza bases have risen and set. Slip the pizzinis off the baking sheet and continue to cook directly on the oven rack for a further 5 minutes until the bases are crisp and golden. Scatter a few basil leaves and some shavings of Parmesan over each pizzini and serve.

# Tasty tuna pan-fried pizza

This pizza requires no proving, as I use a scone-style base that you can fry in the pan. It's quick, simple and very tasty. Don't forget, anything goes, so just change the topping to suit the contents of your fridge and store-cupboard.

**PREPARATION: 15 minutes  COOKING TIME: 20 minutes**

## SERVES 2

**FOR THE TOMATO SAUCE**

1 tablespoon olive oil

2 garlic cloves, finely chopped

2 salad onions, finely chopped

200 g can chopped tomatoes

handful of fresh basil, roughly torn

1 tablespoon tomato ketchup

salt and freshly ground black pepper

**FOR THE TOPPING**

200 g can tuna in olive oil, drained and flaked into chunks

1 red onion, thinly sliced

75 g (3 oz) black olives

75 g (3 oz) mozzarella or Cheddar, diced

**FOR THE DOUGH**

225 g (8 oz) self-raising flour

pinch of salt

2 tablespoons freshly grated Parmesan

150 ml (¼ pint) warm water

2 tablespoons olive oil, plus extra for drizzling

## METHOD

**1** Heat the oil in a small pan and cook the garlic and onions for 2–3 minutes until softened. Stir in the tomatoes, basil, ketchup and a little seasoning. Bring to the boil and simmer for 5–10 minutes until pulpy.

**2** Sift the flour and salt into a large bowl, then stir in the cheese. Make a well in the centre and pour in the water and 1 tablespoon of olive oil. Mix into a soft dough, then roll out into a 25 cm (10 inch) circle.

**3** Heat 1 tablespoon of olive oil in a 25 cm (10 inch) skillet and cook the dough for 5–6 minutes until the underside is golden brown. While the dough is cooking, spoon over the tomato sauce and scatter over the topping ingredients. Drizzle over a little olive oil and place under a preheated grill for 3–4 minutes until the top is golden and the base is cooked through. Cut into wedges and serve with lots of leafy salad.

# Premier pistou-pasta

You know what it's like: late in from work or fancy a quick lunch, well…a touch of French pistou blended with some al dente Italian pasta and you have the perfect answer on a plate that's refreshingly tasty and healthy. Some Rocket and Roast Onion Salad (page 120) served on the side would be a perfect addition.

**PREPARATION: 10 minutes  COOKING TIME: 15 minutes**

## SERVES 4

300 g (11 oz) spaghetti or fettucine

grated rind and juice of 1 lemon

small bunch of fresh flat-leaf parsley

1 tablespoon capers

50 g (2 oz) small, sweet black olives

a pinch of crushed chilli flakes

4 tablespoons olive oil

1 large garlic clove

salt and freshly ground black pepper

Parmesan cheese, to serve

## METHOD

1  Cook the pasta in a large pan of boiling, salted water according to packet instructions.

2  Meanwhile, put the rind and juice from the lemon into a large serving bowl. Roughly chop the parsley and capers and add to the bowl with the olives, chilli flakes and oil.

3  Crush in the garlic and season well.

4  Drain the pasta well and add to the bowl, tossing to mix. Shave or grate over some Parmesan and serve out at the table; remember to set out extra side bowls for spitting out the olive stones.

# Paper potato pizza

A potato pizza sounds a little strange, but wait until you try it and you'll discover how delicious it is. Cut into thin wedges and serve warm or cold with Rocket and Roast Onion Salad (page 120) – although, I've never had it cold 'cos there's never any left.

**PREPARATION: 20 minutes  COOKING TIME: 20 minutes**

## SERVES 4

150 g pack pizza-base mix

1 tablespoon olive oil

flour, for kneading

**FOR THE TOPPING**

250 g (9 oz) red-skinned or new potatoes

2 tablespoons olive oil, plus extra for drizzling

1 teaspoon fresh rosemary leaves

2 garlic cloves, crushed

sea salt and freshly ground black pepper

## METHOD

**1** Pre-heat the oven to 220°C/425°F/Gas 7. Place the pizza-base mix in a large bowl and stir in the olive oil and enough warm water (about 120 ml/ 4 fl oz) to make a soft dough. Knead vigorously on a lightly floured surface for about 5 minutes until smooth and elastic.

**2** Roll the dough out to make a thin 30 cm (12 inch) circle. Transfer to a large baking sheet and set aside in a warm place for 5 minutes or so to rise.

**3** Meanwhile, thinly slice the potatoes using a mandoline, food processor or the side of a box grater. Toss with the oil, rosemary, garlic and some salt and pepper.

**4** Arrange the potato slices on the dough and bake for 10 minutes until risen and set. Slip off the baking sheet and continue to cook directly on the oven rack for a further 10 minutes until crisp and golden.

**5** Drizzle over a little oil, scatter over some sea salt and a good grinding of black pepper. Cut into thin wedges and serve.

**TRY THIS:** Scatter over some thinly sliced pancetta, diced smoked bacon, Parmesan shavings or rocket leaves.

Paper potato pizza

# Baked penne
## with chorizo and Taleggio

Now this will tickle those taste buds. Baking pasta with cheese like this gives a really hearty, warming meal. Taleggio has a lovely flavour, but you could use Camembert or Port Salut instead. I've added chorizo, the spicy Spanish sausage that's flavoured with paprika: as it cooks, it releases its lovely juices into the dish. Absolutely scrumptious! Serve with a nice leafy salad drizzled with olive oil and splashed with your favourite balsamic vinegar.

**PREPARATION: 15 minutes  COOKING TIME: 15 minutes**

## SERVES 4

300 g (11 oz) penne

250 g carton mascarpone

2 teaspoons wholegrain mustard

4 salad onions, thickly sliced

250 g (9 oz) chorizo sausage, cut into chunks

200 g (7 oz) diced Taleggio cheese

salt and freshly ground black pepper

## METHOD

**1** Cook the pasta in a large pan of boiling, salted water according to the packet instructions.

**2** Pre-heat the oven to 200°C/400°F/Gas 6. Drain the pasta well and return to the pan. Mix in the mascarpone and mustard, stirring until the mascarpone melts and coats the penne.

**3** Stir in the salad onions, chorizo and cheese and season, then turn the mixture into an ovenproof dish. Bake for about 15–20 minutes until the top is crisp and golden brown.

# Buttered slam jackets

It really is hard to beat jacket potatoes when it comes to warming, nutritious and economical food. They make great accompaniments to a main meal, and with a tasty filling are satisfying by themselves. Begin by choosing a good main-crop potato, such as a King Edward or Desirée, as they have a desirable floury texture once cooked. If you like a soft skin on your potato, rub a little olive oil into the surface before baking; if you prefer a crunchier skin, leave the potato in the oven for 20 minutes or so longer. For extra-quick jackets, start in the microwave on high power for 8 minutes, then crisp up in a hot oven for 10–15 minutes.

You can bake new potatoes but you'll get a very different result as the flesh is firm and waxy. Rub baby new potatoes with oil and sprinkle with sea salt. Bake, then serve with, for example, my Lovely Tomato Chutney (page 138) or a cheesy fondue-style sauce for dipping into.

Whatever filling or topping I plan to serve my potatoes with, I always start with a knob of butter and a sprinkling of salt.

**PREPARATION: 5 minutes  COOKING TIME: 1½ hours**

## SERVES 1

1 large potato, weighing around 250 g (9 oz)

1 teaspoon olive oil

sea salt

small knob of butter

## METHOD

**1** Pre-heat the oven to 200°C/400°F/Gas 6. Scrub the potato and dry thoroughly. Prick in several places with a fork and rub in the olive oil; sprinkle lightly with sea salt. Bake for 1½ hours until the potato feels soft when gently squeezed.

**2** Wrap the potato in a clean towel and slam down on to a board; alternatively, place the potato on a serving plate with a tea towel on top and hit it with your fist. Both these slamming methods work really well because the force breaks up the potato into fluffy grains and usually causes a natural split.

**3** Drop the butter into the split and sprinkle in a little more salt. Eat immediately or serve with your choice of topping: Here are some of my favourites:
• soured cream and chives
• tuna and garlic mayo
• cream cheese and smoked salmon
• curried baked beans with mature Cheddar
• sautéed leeks, cream cheese and black pepper

# Aubergine chilli jackets

My vegetarian friends simply love this recipe. It's quick, nutritious and extremely satisfying. For a touch of class, I like to serve it with a dollop of soured cream.

**PREPARATION: 15 minutes  COOKING TIME: 25 minutes**

## SERVES 4

2 tablespoons olive oil

1 onion, roughly chopped

2 garlic cloves, roughly chopped

1 red chilli, roughly chopped

2 large aubergines, cubed

2 teaspoons chopped fresh rosemary

150 ml (¼ pint) red wine

400 g can chopped plum tomatoes

400 g can cannellini beans, drained

sea salt and freshly ground black pepper

4 jacket potatoes (page 102)

## METHOD

**1** Heat the oil in a sauté pan and cook the onion, garlic and chilli for 2 minutes over a moderate heat. Add the aubergines and rosemary and continue to cook for a further 4–5 minutes until beginning to soften

**2** Pour in the wine and bring to the boil. Add the tomatoes and beans, season to taste, then cover and cook for 20–25 minutes or so, stirring from time to time.

**3** Divide between hot, buttered jacket potatoes and serve straight away.

# Fluffed, puffed cheese
## and honey ham jackets

These jacket potatoes are a big hit in my house, especially with the children. The combination of honeyed ham and smoked mozzarella is absolutely delicious. Needless to say, ketchup is never requested...

**PREPARATION: 15 minutes  COOKING TIME: 20 minutes**

## SERVES 4

4 jacket potatoes (page 102)

knob of butter

1 tablespoon Dijon mustard

2 eggs, separated

100 g (4 oz) smoked mozzarella, diced

75 g (3 oz) honey-roast ham, roughly chopped

3 tablespoons snipped fresh chives

salt and freshly ground black pepper

green-leaf salad, to serve

## METHOD

**1** After taking the cooked potatoes out of the oven, lower the temperature to 180°C/350°F/Gas 4. Cut a 1 cm (½ inch) slice off the top of each potato and scoop out the flesh to leave a 5 mm (¼ inch) thick shell.

**2** Mash the flesh with the butter, mustard and egg yolks. Stir in the cheese, ham, chives and some salt and pepper.

**3** Whisk the egg whites until fairly stiff and fold into the potato mixture. Pile back into the shells and bake for 20 minutes until puffed and lightly browned. Serve hot with a crisp green-leaf salad.

Fluffed, puffed cheese and honey ham jackets

# Jacqueline's potato skins
## with guacamole

Crispy skins like these make really great party food, as well as an appetizing side dish. Serve them with a bowl of guacamole and also the soured cream dip from my Baconeese Cream Potato Wedges on page 108. The potato flesh can be saved and used to make my delicious Grate Hash Browns (page 113) for breakfast or brunch the next day. My sister Jacqueline likes to add a portion of the potato to her guacamole. It really works a treat, but you must mix it in well – ideally, using a food processor.

**PREPARATION: 15 minutes  COOKING TIME: 20 minutes**

## SERVES 2

2 jacket potatoes (page 102)

2 tablespoons olive oil

coarse sea salt

**FOR THE GUACAMOLE**

1 large, ripe avocado, halved and stoned

1 garlic clove, crushed

1 red chilli, seeded and finely chopped

2 tablespoons chopped fresh coriander

juice of 1 lime

salt and freshly ground black pepper

## METHOD

**1** Bake the potatoes as described on page 102. Raise the oven temperature to 220°C/425°F/Gas 7. Halve the potatoes and scoop out the flesh to leave a 5 mm (¼ inch) thick shell. Cut each half into 3–4 strips, place in a bowl and toss with the oil.

**2** Arrange the strips, skin-side down, on a sturdy baking sheet. Sprinkle with coarse sea salt and bake for 20 minutes or so until the strips are crisp and golden brown.

**3** Next, make the guacamole: place the avocado flesh in a bowl and mash with a fork until fairly smooth. Stir in the garlic, chilli and coriander.

**4** Add lime juice and salt and pepper to taste. Transfer to a bowl and serve with the crispy skins.

**CHEF'S TIP:** If you have any guacamole left over, squeeze fresh lemon or lime juice over it and cover with plastic wrap to help prevent discolouration.

# Breaking bubble and Savoy squeak

Like Granny's Corned-Beef Hash and Fried Egg on page 85, this is also a quick, throw-it-together dish. It's great on its own with a steak or fried egg, but best of all, throw in some crispy bacon or diced spicy chorizo for a supper treat in front of the box.

**PREPARATION: 15 minutes  COOKING TIME: 20 minutes**

## SERVES 2

350 g (12 oz) floury potatoes, diced

half a small Savoy cabbage, shredded

2 tablespoons vegetable oil

1 small onion, chopped

2 garlic cloves, crushed

2 red chillies, thinly sliced

2 teaspoons Worcestershire or soy sauce

salt and freshly ground black pepper

## METHOD

**1** Cook the potatoes in a large pan of boiling, salted water for 8 minutes. Add the cabbage and cook for a further 3–4 minutes until tender.

**2** Meanwhile, heat the oil in a large frying-pan and cook the onion, garlic and chillies for 5 minutes until golden.

**3** Drain the potatoes and cabbage well and add to the frying-pan. Crush with a wooden spoon, then leave the mixture to cook over a medium heat for 2–3 minutes until a crust forms on the bottom.

**4** Break up the mixture, stir in the Worcestershire or soy sauce and season, then leave to cook again until a crust forms on the bottom; break up again and cook for a third time. Spoon on to plates and serve.

**CHEF'S TIP:** Leave out the chilli if you're feeding this to kids.

# Baconeese
## cream potato wedges

The combination of bacon, cheese and potato is perfect. Add a chopped salad onion and soured cream and you're in heaven. I like to serve these wedges on the side with – and I know it sounds odd – the Classic Moules Marinière on page 65; they really taste fab together. Of course, you can serve them with all manner of other things, or on their own for a tasty snack.

**PREPARATION: 15 minutes  COOKING TIME: 40 minutes**

### SERVES 4

4 x 250 g (9 oz) baking potatoes

2 tablespoons olive oil

1 teaspoon paprika

½ teaspoon sea salt

75 g (3 oz) streaky bacon, chopped

100 g (4 oz) Gruyère or Cheddar, finely grated

4 salad onions, chopped

### FOR THE DIP

300 ml (½ pint) soured cream

4 salad onions, finely chopped

1 teaspoon horseradish sauce

### METHOD

**1** Pre-heat the oven to 220°C/425°F/Gas 7. Cut each potato into 8 wedges and place in a bowl with the oil, paprika and salt. Toss well together, arrange on a sturdy baking sheet and cook for 20 minutes, turning occasionally. Scatter over the bacon and return to the oven for 10 minutes until the potatoes are cooked through and golden and the bacon is sizzling and crispy.

**2** Scatter over the grated cheese and salad onions and return to the oven for a further 10 minutes until the cheese is melted and bubbly and the wedges are nicely browned.

**3** Meanwhile, make the dip by stirring together the soured cream, salad onions and horseradish sauce. Spoon into a serving bowl, place the bowl into the centre of a large plate and arrange the cheesy wedges around the dip, scraping any cheese and bacon pieces on top of the wedges. Serve hot.

**TRY THIS:** If you have any left-over boiled or baked potatoes, cut them roughly into cubes and toss with the oil and paprika as before. Scatter with bacon and cook for 10 minutes, followed by the cheese for another 10 minutes. Hey presto, a scrumptious hash – great with a fried egg on top!

# Excellent egg and ginger fried rice

The secret to successful egg fried rice is to cook the eggs before you add the rice – it works a treat. With a touch more salad onion and ginger, this rice really titillates those taste buds.

**PREPARATION: 5 minutes  COOKING TIME: 10 minutes**

## SERVES 2

1 tablespoon vegetable oil

4 salad onions, thinly sliced

1 garlic clove, finely chopped

2 cm (¾ inch) piece fresh root ginger, grated or finely chopped

1 egg

175 g (6 oz) cooked long-grain rice

50 g (2 oz) frozen peas

1 tablespoon soy sauce

freshly ground black pepper

## METHOD

**1**  Heat the oil in a wok and cook the salad onions, garlic and ginger for 2 minutes. Crack in the egg and scramble with a chopstick for a couple of minutes until just set.

**2**  Stir in the rice and peas and continue to cook for a further 3–4 minutes until piping hot. Season with soy sauce and a few twists of black pepper and serve.

**CHEF'S TIP:** If I don't have any left-over cooked rice to hand, I use frozen rice. It comes in free-flow bags and works brilliantly in stir-fries and other quick dishes. Buy it at your freezer store or supermarket.

# Perfect golden, crispy chips

People often ask me how to make the perfect chips that are crunchy on the outside and fluffy in the centre. Well, here you have it and you don't even need an electric fryer. Remember to do the bread test for perfect results.

**PREPARATION: 5 minutes  COOKING TIME: 10 minutes**

## SERVES 1

1 large potato

vegetable oil, for frying

cubes of bread, to test oil temperature

salt

## METHOD

**1** Scrub the potato in clean, cold water and cut into fingers as thick or thin as you choose. Wash well to rinse off the excess starch and help prevent them sticking together during cooking. Dry thoroughly with kitchen paper.

**2** Heat 5 cm (2 inches) vegetable oil in a small, deep frying-pan. Test the oil temperature with a cube of bread – it should take 60 seconds to turn brown. When the oil has reached the right temperature – do not let it get too hot – cook the chips for 5 minutes or until pale golden.

**3** Remove with a slotted spoon and drain on kitchen paper. Raise the heat slightly and, when the oil is hot enough to brown a cube of bread in 30 seconds, return the chips to the pan for 1–2 minutes until crisp and golden. Drain on kitchen paper, sprinkle with salt, splash with malt vinegar and eat immediately

# Sesame prawn toasts

Once you've tried these prawn toasties, you'll be making them again and again – they're so easy to do. Great with my Hot and Sour Chicken and Mushroom Soup (page 46), they also make a fantastic, very attractive and quick snack. Now that's what I call impressive.

**PREPARATION: 10 minutes  COOKING TIME: 5 minutes**

## SERVES 4

175 g (6 oz) cooked peeled prawns

2 cm (¾ inch) piece fresh root ginger, grated

1 garlic clove, finely chopped

1 egg white

2 teaspoons cornflour

¼ teaspoon Chinese five-spice powder

¼ teaspoon salt

4 thin slices of bread, crusts removed

2 tablespoons sesame seeds

vegetable oil, for shallow-frying

## METHOD

**1** Place the prawns, ginger and garlic in a mini chopper or food processor and whizz until finely minced.

**2** Whisk the egg white until frothy, then stir in the prawn mixture, cornflour, Chinese five-spice powder and salt until well blended.

**3** Spread the mixture evenly on to the bread, then sprinkle over the sesame seeds, pressing them in firmly with the fingertips. Cut each slice into 4 squares, fingers or triangles.

**4** Heat about 3–4 tablespoons of oil in a frying-pan; when hot, reduce the heat before adding the toasts. Cook prawn-side down for 2–3 minutes until golden, then turn and cook the other side – you might need a little more oil. Drain on kitchen paper and serve warm.

# Grate hash browns

For a tasty treat, these hash browns are a perfect snack on their own. But I often make them for a weekend brunch served with my favourite sausages and cheesy baked beans.

**PREPARATION: 5 minutes  COOKING TIME: 25 minutes**

## SERVES 2

2 small, floury potatoes

salt and freshly ground black pepper

vegetable oil, for frying

## METHOD

**1** Cook the whole potatoes in a pan of boiling, salted water for 15 minutes until just tender. Drain and cool slightly.

**2** Coarsely grate the potatoes into a bowl and season generously. Firmly shape the mixture into 4 oval patties by patting the mixture together with the palms of your hands.

**3** Heat a little oil in a large frying-pan and cook the hash browns for 3–4 minutes on each side until crisp and golden. Drain on kitchen paper and serve hot.

**TRY THIS:** Add a nice touch of green with a few fresh chopped herbs – my favourite is thyme.

# Garlic and parsley frittata

A frittata is simply an Italian omelette that you can add all sorts of ingredients to. It has a great taste with a lovely springy texture courtesy of the bread. A white slice will do, but you could be more adventurous. Serve with a watercress salad.

**PREPARATION: 10 minutes  COOKING TIME: 10 minutes**

## SERVES 1

2 tablespoons milk

2 eggs

1 tablespoon chopped fresh parsley

1 garlic clove, crushed

pinch of dried chilli flakes (optional)

1 slice white bread, torn into small pieces

sea salt and freshly ground black pepper

1 tablespoon olive oil

1 tablespoon freshly grated Parmesan

watercress salad, to serve

## METHOD

1  Beat together the milk, eggs, parsley, garlic and chilli flakes, if using. Add the torn bread and some salt and pepper; set aside for 5 minutes so that the bread completely softens into the mixture.

2  Heat the oil in a 20 cm (8 inch) frying-pan and pour in the egg mixture. Cook for 3 minutes or so until golden and almost set.

3  Slide the frittata on to a plate, then turn the pan over on top of the plate and carefully flip over so you can cook the other side. Scatter over the Parmesan. Cook for a further couple of minutes until the underside is golden, the cheese has melted and the frittata is cooked through. Serve with a fresh, crisp watercress salad and a glass of your favourite Chianti.

# Tabletop naan
## with spicy fried onions

I've often eaten this in Indian restaurants, and it's always so yummy, with such a great taste and texture. I've put together a recipe for making it yourself and it's certainly worth the effort.

**PREPARATION: 30 minutes  COOKING TIME: 25 minutes**

## SERVES 2

450 g (1 lb) plain flour

pinch of salt

½ teaspoon baking powder

¼ teaspoon bicarbonate of soda

1 teaspoon caster sugar

1 egg

150 g carton natural yoghurt

4 tablespoons milk

2 tablespoons vegetable oil

25 g (1 oz) butter, melted

**FOR THE SPICY ONIONS**

2 tablespoons vegetable oil

2 onions, thinly sliced

2 teaspoons garam masala

½ teaspoon caster sugar

½ teaspoon table salt

## METHOD

**1** Pre-heat the oven to 220°C/425°F/Gas 7. Sift the flour, salt, baking powder and bicarbonate of soda into a bowl. Stir in the sugar.

**2** In a separate bowl, whisk together the egg, yoghurt, milk and oil. Pour into the flour mixture and bring together to make a soft dough. Knead briefly, cover with oiled plastic wrap and set aside for 15 minutes.

**3** For the spicy onions, heat the oil in a pan and cook the onions with the garam masala, sugar and salt for 15 minutes until golden brown.

**4** Roll the dough out into a large rectangle. Using your fingers, press the dough into a swiss-roll tin. Scatter over the spicy onions, pressing them into the surface of the dough with the back of a spoon. Bake for 10 minutes until puffed and browned. Remove, brush with the melted butter and serve warm.

# Green onion chapatis

I find chapatis really useful. They're easy to make and you can add all manner of extra flavourings – in this case salad onions. They're wonderful with curries, and the perfect accompaniment for many other dishes. You can buy chapati flour, basically a very fine flour, from an Indian grocer, but otherwise, use half ordinary wholemeal and half plain flour as I have done here. I stick to the authentic method by not adding any salt, but you can add a little if you prefer.

**PREPARATION: 15 minutes  COOKING TIME: 15 minutes**

## MAKES 12

150 g (5 oz) plain flour, plus extra for dusting

150 g (5 oz) fine wholemeal flour

4 salad onions, very finely chopped

## METHOD

**1** Sift the flours into a large bowl and stir in the salad onions. Gradually add 200 ml (7 fl oz) cold water to make a fairly firm dough. Knead vigorously for 5 minutes, then cover with a damp tea towel and set aside to rest.

**2** Heat a heavy-based frying-pan or griddle, ideally cast-iron, but otherwise non-stick. Divide the dough into 12 balls, dust with flour and roll out into rough 15 cm (6 inch) rounds. Pass the rounds from hand to hand to shake off any excess flour.

**3** Cook each chapati in the hot pan for a minute or so on each side until golden and a little puffed. Stack on a plate and keep covered until all the chapatis are cooked, remembering to wipe out the pan with kitchen paper between each chapati. Serve warm.

**CHEF'S TIP:** Left-over chapatis can be successfully re-heated in the microwave. Sprinkle a little water on each chapati and re-heat on high power for about 20 seconds or so.

# Mozzamary garlic bread

Classic garlic bread with mozzarella cheese and rosemary makes a tasty accompaniment or side dish, but I find it particularly well suited to a bowl of steaming soup, such as the Roasted Tomato and Crème Fraîche Soup on page 42.

**PREPARATION: 10 minutes  COOKING TIME: 20 minutes**

## SERVES 4

150 g ball of mozzarella, drained

50 g (2 oz) butter, at room temperature

2 garlic cloves, crushed

2 teaspoons chopped fresh rosemary

¼ teaspoon salt

freshly ground black pepper

1 baguette

## METHOD

**1** Pre-heat the oven to 200°C/400°F/Gas 6. Roughly chop the mozzarella and place in a food processor with the butter, garlic, rosemary, salt and pepper. Whizz together to form a coarse paste.

**2** Diagonally slice into the baguette at 2.5 cm (1 inch) intervals, taking care not to slice right through the base.

**3** Spread the mozzarella mixture between the slices of bread, smearing any left over across the top.

**4** Wrap the loaf in foil, making sure the ends are well sealed, but leaving the top open so that it can crust up in the oven. Bake for 20 minutes until the butter has melted and the cheese is bubbling; serve immediately.

**CHEF'S TIP:** If the baguette is too long to fit into your oven, just cut into 2 even-lengths and wrap individually.

# Fern's creamy, crispy onion rings

Now here's a Fern favourite I've prepared many a time on *Ready, Steady, Cook,* as it's easy, goes with so many things and presents beautifully. If you have more time than I did — without Fern asking, 'What's in there?' – soak the onions in milk longer for really creamy, crispy onion rings.

**PREPARATION: 5 minutes + soaking time  COOKING TIME: 5 minutes**

## SERVES 2

1 Spanish onion

150 ml (¼ pint) milk

6 tablespoons seasoned flour

vegetable oil, for frying

## METHOD

**1** Slice the onion into 1 cm (½ inch) wide slices, then separate the rings. Place in a bowl with the milk and set aside for 5–30 minutes (depending on how much time you can spare – the longer the better).

**2** Heat 5 cm (2 inches) of vegetable oil in a deep frying-pan.

**3** Drain the onion rings, dust in the seasoned flour, then fry in batches for 2–3 minutes until crisp and golden. Drain on kitchen paper and eat hot.

# Rocket
## and roast onion salad

Roasted onions are absolutely delicious, but you don't see them that often. I like to serve them hot as a side vegetable, but they also make an extra-special salad when tossed with peppery rocket and salty Parmesan or Pecorino.

**PREPARATION: 10 minutes  COOKING TIME: 30 minutes**

## SERVES 4

12 button onions, halved

3 tablespoons olive oil

sea salt and coarsely ground black pepper

1 tablespoon balsamic vinegar

50 g (2 oz) Parmesan or Pecorino

100 g (4 oz) rocket leaves

## METHOD

**1** Pre-heat the oven to 190°C/375°F/Gas 5. Place the onions in a shallow roasting tin and drizzle over the oil. Season generously and roast for 25–30 minutes until the onions are softened and nicely browned.

**2** Drizzle over the balsamic vinegar and allow the onions to cool to room temperature.

**3** Using a swivel-style peeler, shave the cheese into wafer-thin slices.

**4** Arrange the rocket, roast onions and cheese on 4 serving plates; drizzle round the pan juices and serve.

# Pulao rice

Rice makes the perfect accompaniment to many Indian dishes, such as my tasty Lightning Lamb Dhansak (page 86). I've kept my pulao rice quite simple so that it doesn't mask the flavour of the curry you're serving with it.

**PREPARATION: 20 minutes  COOKING TIME: 25 minutes**

## SERVES 6

4 tablespoons vegetable oil

3 onions, thinly sliced

1 cinnamon stick

1 teaspoon cumin seeds

3 cardamom pods, cracked

3 star anise

500 g (1 lb 2 oz) basmati rice, rinsed

2 teaspoons salt

handful fresh coriander leaves

## METHOD

**1** Heat the oil in a large pan and cook half the onions over a fairly high heat for about 10 minutes until crisp and lightly browned. Drain on kitchen paper and set aside, leaving just a coating of oil still in the pan.

**2** Add the remaining onions to the pan with the cinnamon, cumin, cardamom and star anise and cook gently for 5 minutes or so until the onions are golden.

**3** Add the rice, cook for 1 minute, then add 1 litre (1¾ pints) of cold water and the salt. Bring to the boil, cover and cook over a low heat for 12 minutes until the grains are tender and the water has been absorbed.

**4** Remove from the heat and leave to stand, covered, for 5 minutes. Transfer to a serving dish and scatter over the fried onions and coriander leaves; serve warm.

# Warm sweet potato
## and roast tomato cheese salad

A lovely combination of flavours that works surprisingly well and has instantly become a favourite among friends.

**PREPARATION: 15 minutes  COOKING TIME: 40 minutes**

## SERVES 4

500 g (1 lb 2 oz) sweet potatoes, cubed

1 garlic bulb, broken into cloves

3 tablespoons olive oil

1 teaspoon cumin seeds

8 fresh basil leaves, shredded

sea salt and freshly ground black pepper

4 small vines of cherry tomatoes, each with about 5 tomatoes

75 g (3 oz) strong blue cheese, e.g. Gorgonzola or Stilton

1 tablespoon red wine vinegar

## METHOD

**1** Pre heat the oven to 200°C/400°F/Gas 6. Toss together the sweet potatoes, garlic, 1 tablespoon of the oil, the cumin seeds, basil and some salt and pepper.

**2** Arrange on a baking sheet or shallow roasting tin and cook for 25 minutes. Add the tomato vines, trying to keep them intact – if there's not enough room in the tin, place the tomatoes on a separate baking sheet. Drizzle over a little more oil and cook for a further 15 minutes until the tomatoes are softened.

**3** Lift off the tomatoes and set aside. Pile the sweet potatoes on to 4 serving plates and scatter over the crumbled blue cheese. Place a tomato vine on top of each and drizzle round a little more oil and a splash of red wine vinegar. Serve warm.

# Spicy Spanish patatas bravas

Based on authentic *patatas bravas*, which translates as 'wild potatoes', this dish contains spices that certainly give a fiery flavour, while the cooking aroma gets the juices flowing early. Serve with a bowl of garlic mayonnaise or some of my Lovely Tomato Chutney (page 138).

**PREPARATION: 10 minutes  COOKING TIME: 40 minutes**

## SERVES 4

500 g (1 lb 2 oz) baby new potatoes

2 tablespoons olive oil

2 teaspoons paprika

2 teaspoons chilli powder

1 teaspoon ground cumin

1 teaspoon sea salt

1 tablespoon finely chopped fresh parsley

## METHOD

**1** Pre-heat the oven to 200°C/400°F/Gas 6. Place the potatoes in a strong plastic bag and bash with a rolling pin to crack them. Add the oil, paprika, chilli powder, cumin, sea salt and parsley to the bag, then shake well to mix.

**2** Empty the potatoes on to a baking sheet and spread out into a single layer. Roast for 40 minutes, shaking the tray occasionally, until cooked through and nicely browned.

# Minted
# mushy chip-shop peas

OK, so you could just open a can – but home-made mushy peas really are terrific (and don't need to be that lurid green). I love to serve them with my Deep-fried Cod in Beer Batter (page 57) and Perfect Golden, Crispy Chips (page 111). Soaking the peas takes a little time, but after that this recipe is really quick, easy and so much cheaper than the canned variety.

**PREPARATION: 2 hours  COOKING TIME: 20 minutes**

## SERVES 6

250 g (9 oz) quick-soak dried peas

1 teaspoon sea salt

4 tablespoons malt vinegar

1 tablespoon mint sauce

sea salt and freshly ground black pepper

## METHOD

1 Soak the peas for 2 hours or according to the packet instructions.

2 Drain the peas and place in a pan with 450 ml (¾ pint) of cold water. Bring to the boil and simmer for 20 minutes until the mixture is tender and thickened.

3 Stir in the salt, vinegar and mint sauce, and season to taste. Serve warm.

**CHEF'S TIP:** Left over mushy peas keep very well for a few days, covered, in the fridge. Re-heat in the microwave.

# Hail Caesar salad

The original dressing for this didn't contain anchovies as is commonly thought, so those of you who don't like them needn't miss out. Just sit back and enjoy this classic, which will be around for ever. Hail Caesar!

**PREPARATION: 15 minutes**

## SERVES 4-6

1 cos lettuce

6–8 tinned anchovies, chopped

100 g (4 oz) Parmesan, grated

### FOR THE DRESSING

1 large egg

1 garlic clove, roughly chopped

juice of 1 lime or ½ lemon

2 teaspoons English mustard powder

few shakes of Worcestershire sauce

150 ml (¼ pint) olive oil

sea salt and freshly ground black pepper

## METHOD

**1** Make the dressing: place the egg in a food processor with the garlic, lime or lemon juice, mustard powder and Worcestershire sauce. With the motor running, slowly pour in the oil to make a smooth sauce about the thickness of single cream. Season to taste and chill until ready to serve.

**2** To make a classic Caesar salad, tear up the lettuce leaves and mix with the chopped anchovies and grated Parmesan. Drizzle with the dressing and scatter over a few Roasted Parmesan Croûtons (page 128).

**TRY THIS:** The dressing also tastes great drizzled over chicken or large grilled prawns.

# Roasted Parmesan croûtons

These cheesy croûtons are really useful for tossing into bowls of soup and scattering over salads – they add flavour and that all-important crunch. I find that cooking them in the oven gives an even browning and means you can add less oil than when frying them.

**PREPARATION: 5 minutes  COOKING TIME: 10 minutes**

## SERVES 2

2 thick slices country-style bread

1 tablespoon olive oil

1 tablespoon finely grated Parmesan

1 garlic clove, crushed

salt and freshly ground black pepper

## METHOD

**1** Pre-heat the oven to 190°C/375°F/Gas 5. Slice the crusts off the bread and discard. Cut the bread into cubes and toss with the olive oil, Parmesan, garlic and salt and pepper. Scatter on to a baking sheet and cook in the oven for 10 minutes until crisp and golden.

**2** Allow to cool a little, then serve.

**TRY THIS:** Ciabatta and flavoured focaccia, such as those made with olives or sun-dried tomato, make fantastic croûtons.

# New millennium posh potato salad

I like to serve my new potato salad while it's still a little warm, but it's nearly as good after a day in the fridge. You can't beat a warm potato salad like this – it's totally comforting and, once on the table, is always the first salad to disappear, so make plenty.

**PREPARATION: 15 minutes  COOKING TIME: 10 minutes**

## SERVES 6

500 g (1 lb 2 oz) baby new potatoes, halved

75 g (3 oz) cubed pancetta or lardons

1 garlic clove, crushed

4 anchovies in oil, drained

4 tablespoons mayonnaise

4 salad onions, thinly sliced

salt and freshly ground black pepper

## METHOD

**1** Cook the potatoes in a pan of boiling, salted water for 10 minutes or so, until just tender.

**2** Meanwhile, cook the pancetta in a non-stick frying-pan for 3–4 minutes until crisp and golden brown; drain on kitchen paper.

**3** Drain the potatoes in a colander and leave to cool a while.

**4** Make the dressing: mash together the garlic and anchovies then mix with the mayo. Toss with the warm potatoes, salad onions and crispy bacon, season with pepper and serve.

# Citrus couscous and sultana salad

For a vegetarian treat, you simply can't beat this audacious salad with its wonderful colours, textures and flavour, which make it absolutely delicious.

**PREPARATION: 20 minutes**

## SERVES 4

175 g (6 oz) couscous

300 ml (½ pint) hot vegetable stock

grated rind and juice of 1 lemon

2 small garlic cloves

200 g carton Greek yoghurt

a pinch of caster sugar

salt and freshly ground black pepper

3 tablespoons olive oil

1 red onion, finely chopped

400 g can chick peas, drained and rinsed

2 tablespoons roughly chopped fresh coriander, plus sprigs to garnish

50g (2 oz) small sultanas

## METHOD

**1** Place the couscous in a large heatproof bowl and pour over the hot stock, then add the lemon rind and juice. Set aside for 10 minutes or so until the liquid has been absorbed.

**2** Meanwhile, crush the garlic cloves into the yoghurt, add the sugar and season to taste; set aside.

**3** Using a fork, lightly stir the couscous to separate the grains, then gently mix in the olive oil, onion, chick peas, coriander and sultanas. Add salt and pepper to taste. At this stage the salad can be chilled until ready to serve.

**4** Divide the salad between 4 side bowls and spoon some of the garlic yoghurt on top of each. Lightly ripple it through the top of the salad, then garnish each bowl with a coriander sprig.

# Maddie's mango chutney

This is a simple chutney with a lovely flavour that develops over time. It's worth the effort of making it yourself as it's so much nicer than commercially made varieties. Keep it in the fridge – I can't tell you how long it will store because it always gets eaten way too quickly in my house. Ask my daughter Maddie…

**PREPARATION: 20 minutes  COOKING TIME: 40 minutes**

## MAKES 900 ml (1½ pints)

4 garlic cloves, roughly chopped

2.5 cm (1 inch) piece root ginger, coarsely grated

1 red chilli, seeded and roughly chopped

½ teaspoon ground turmeric

1 teaspoon cayenne pepper

350 ml (12 fl oz) white wine vinegar

2 large green mangoes, cut into 2 cm (¾ inch) cubes

1 teaspoon salt

400 g (14 oz) golden caster sugar

4 tablespoons sultanas

1 star anise

## METHOD

**1** Place the garlic, ginger, chilli, turmeric, cayenne and a splash of the vinegar in a mini-chopper or food processor and blitz to a smooth paste.

**2** Put the paste in a large pan with the remaining vinegar, the mangoes, salt, sugar, sultanas and star anise. Bring to the boil and simmer for 1 hour or so until the mixture has thickened – don't worry if it stills looks a little watery, as it will thicken further on cooling. Pour into a clean jar, seal and allow to cool. Now, where's that ham sandwich?

# Easy mint chutney

If you like a bit on the side, this delicious relish goes with all manner of starters and curries. Try it with Sage and Onion Bhajis (page 8), Celtic Samosas (page 9) and Crispy Crunchy Sweetcorn Fritters (page 39). Any left-over chutney can be stirred into natural yoghurt and served with poppadoms and strips of toasted pitta. Or why not make it to go with that take-away curry you've just ordered?

**PREPARATION: 5 minutes**

## SERVES 4

4 mild green chillies, seeded and roughly chopped

25 g (1 oz) fresh mint, chopped

15 g (½ oz) fresh coriander, chopped

2 teaspoons caster sugar

1 teaspoon garam masala

½ teaspoon table salt

juice of 1 lemon

## METHOD

**1** Place the chillies, mint and coriander in a mini food processor or liquidizer and whizz until very finely chopped. You might need to stop the food processor from time to time and give the mixture a stir.

**2** Add the sugar, garam masala, salt, lemon juice and a tablespoon or two of water. Whizz again until smooth, then chill until ready to serve.

**CHEF'S TIP:** As always, when using fresh, raw herbs, try not to make this too far ahead of time as the colour will fade.

# Ainsley's curry sauce to go

It doesn't matter whether you're from Yorkshire or Yarmouth, you can't beat the taste of curry sauce with chips. When I'm making chips at home (see page 111), it's too much trouble to go out just for the sauce, so this is my own version and I think it's just like the real thing – dead gorgeous!

**PREPARATION: 10 minutes  COOKING TIME: 15 minutes**

## SERVES 4

1 tablespoon vegetable oil

1 onion, finely chopped

1 red apple, roughly chopped

300 ml (½ pint) vegetable stock

1 tablespoon curry paste

1 tablespoon cornflour

2 tablespoons frozen peas

2 tablespoons fruity brown sauce

salt and freshly ground black pepper

## METHOD

**1** Heat the oil in a pan and cook the onion and apple for 3–4 minutes until softened and beginning to brown. Stir in the stock and curry paste and simmer together for 5 minutes.

**2** Dissolve the cornflour in a little water and stir into the sauce with the peas and brown sauce. Bring to the boil and simmer for 2–3 minutes. Season to taste and serve warm (preferably over freshly fried chips).

**TRY THIS:** I think the fruity brown sauce is the secret to the success of this recipe, but if you don't have any, try it with regular brown sauce or a tablespoon of sandwich pickle.

# Real tartare sauce

It's really easy (and a lot nicer) to make your own tartare sauce using shop-bought mayonnaise rather than forking out the premium price charged for a jar of it. Yes, you might have to go out and buy your capers, gherkins and a few other items, but once made, it will keep in the fridge for a day or two. Calamari, whitebait and fried fish of any kind all taste great with a spoonful on the side.

**PREPARATION: 10 minutes**

## SERVES 8

200 g jar mayonnaise

1 shallot, very finely chopped

2 tablespoons pickled capers, well rinsed and roughly chopped

2 gherkins, roughly chopped

2 teaspoons horseradish sauce

1 teaspoon English mustard

3 tablespoons finely chopped fresh parsley

## METHOD

Mix all the ingredients together. Cover and chill until ready to serve.

**TRY THIS!** Add a squeeze of fresh lemon juice for an extra kick, or a sprinkling of cayenne pepper for an extra, extra kick.

# Lovely tomato chutney

This is a really versatile chutney. I love it in a nice cheesy toasted sandwich, on the side with a ploughman's lunch, or dolloped on top of my Wrap and Roll Hot Dogs (page 22). Ooh, lovely!

**PREPARATION: 10 minutes  COOKING TIME: 60 minutes**

## MAKES 850 g (1 lb 14 oz)

1 kg (2¼ lb) ripe tomatoes, roughly chopped

1 large onion, chopped

3 garlic cloves, finely chopped

150 ml (¼ pint) white wine vinegar

200 g (7 oz) light brown sugar

1 teaspoon salt

½ teaspoon dried chilli flakes

4 cardamom pods, cracked

¼ teaspoon ground cinnamon

## METHOD

**1**  Place all the ingredients in a large pan. Bring to the boil and simmer for 60 minutes, stirring fairly frequently until thickened and pulpy.

**2**  Remove from the heat and stir occasionally until cool, then pour into a clean jar, seal and allow to cool completely.

Char-grilled vegetables and hummus ciabatta *with* Lovely tomato chutney

# Banana raita

This gorgeous raita is so refreshing and is the perfect accompaniment to curry and spicy dishes. My wife likes to make it just before the take-away arrives.

**PREPARATION: 5 minutes**

## SERVES 2

1 ripe banana

1 garlic clove, crushed

150 g carton natural yoghurt

juice of ½ lemon

¼ teaspoon salt

## METHOD

Mash the banana well with a fork and mix with the garlic and yoghurt. Add lemon juice and salt to taste. Serve immediately.

# Red onion relish

This relish is particularly nice scattered on top of a plain salad, or equally delicious in a cheesy tomato sandwich. To toast the cumin seeds, use a dry frying-pan set over a medium heat and cook them for 2–3 minutes, stirring all the time.

**PREPARATION: 15 minutes**

## SERVES 4

2 red onions, thinly sliced

½ teaspoon table salt

½ teaspoon cumin seeds, toasted

2 tablespoons red wine vinegar

1 red chilli, seeded and finely chopped

1 teaspoon caster sugar

2 tablespoons chopped coriander

## METHOD

**1** Place the red onions in a bowl. Sprinkle over the salt and set aside for 10 minutes.

**2** Pat the onions dry and mix with the remaining ingredients. Chill until ready to serve.

# Soy dipping sauces

I've got two favourite ways of making this – the first one is a little more fiery than the other. As you get used to the flavours, you can adjust the quantities to suit your taste.

## Floating chilli soy dipping sauce

For this you need to use an authentic chilli oil from an oriental grocer. This contains shrimp paste, so it has more depth than a Mediterranean-style chilli oil, which is normally just olive oil and chillies.

**PREPARATION: 2 minutes**

### SERVES 2

4 tablespoons soy sauce

1 teaspoon rice vinegar or white wine vinegar

¼ teaspoon chilli oil

pinch of chilli flakes (optional)

### METHOD

Mix all the ingredients together well and serve. The chilli flakes are optional, but look and taste wonderful.

## Sweet soy sesame dipping sauce

**Preparation: 5 minutes**

### SERVES 4

3 tablespoons soy sauce

2 tablespoons sake or dry sherry

1 tablespoon brown sugar

½ teaspoon sesame seeds

### METHOD

Mix all the ingredients together, stirring until the sugar dissolves.

# Sweet chilli sauce

I usually make up big batches of this and keep it in the fridge because it's so handy for adding to other dishes for a little extra heat and sweetness – and, of course, it's a great accompaniment to all kinds of dishes, such as Celtic Samosas (page 9), Crispy Cache Calamari (page 69) and Pacific Prawn Fu-yung (page 56).

**PREPARATION: 5 minutes  COOKING TIME: 5 minutes**

## SERVES 4

1 tablespoon sunflower oil

1 onion, chopped

2 garlic cloves, finely chopped

2 red chillies, finely chopped

juice of 1 orange

1 tablespoon clear honey

1 tablespoon malt vinegar

2 tablespoons tomato ketchup

## METHOD

**1** Heat the oil in a small pan and cook the onion for 2–3 minutes over a medium heat.

**2** Add the garlic and chillies and continue to cook for a further 2 minutes, stirring occasionally, until softened.

**3** Stir in the orange juice, honey, vinegar and tomato ketchup and heat through gently until just beginning to bubble. Remove from the heat, cool slightly and serve.

# Mama Tahsia's tzatziki

Tzatziki is a Greek classic, so refreshing on the palate, and perfect for jazzing up kebabs, salads and my recipe for Dimitri's Festive Feta Triangles (page 36).

**PREPARATION: 10 minutes**

## SERVES 4

½ cucumber

200 g carton Greek yoghurt

4 tablespoons chopped fresh mint

2 garlic cloves, crushed

pinch of dried oregano

pinch of caster sugar

juice of 1 lime

salt and freshly ground black pepper

## METHOD

Grate the cucumber into a sieve set over a bowl, or finely dice. Try to avoid using the central seeded core as it's very watery. Squeeze out any excess water by presssing the cucumber down into the sieve and transfer to a bowl. Add the yoghurt, mint, garlic, oregano, caster sugar and lime juice. Season to taste and chill until ready to use. Garnish with a sprig of mint and serve with olives and triangles of pitta bread.

# Portuguese custard tarts

This is one of the best ways I know to finish off a sunny lunch – brilliant with an espresso.

**PREPARATION: 20 minutes  COOKING TIME: 20 minutes**

## MAKES 16

75 g (3 oz) golden caster sugar

2 tablespoons cornflour

450 ml (¾ pint) milk

2 egg yolks

1 teaspoon vanilla extract

375 g pack ready-rolled puff pastry

plain flour for rolling

## METHOD

**1** Place the sugar in a pan with 5 tablespoons of water and gently bring to the boil, stirring until the sugar dissolves.

**2** Dissolve the cornflour in a little of the milk. Whisk the remaining milk, the egg yolks, vanilla extract and cornflour mixture into the sugar syrup. Gently bring to the boil, stirring continuously, until smooth and thickened. Cover the custard and allow to cool.

**3** Open out the sheet of pastry and roll out a little more to a thickness of 3 mm (⅛ inch). Stamp out the pastry into 10 cm (4 inch) circles and use them to line a small bun tin (the pastry might come further up the sides of each tin than usual, but it will shrink as it cooks). Refrigerate until the custard is cool.

**4** Preheat the oven to 200°C/400°F/Gas 6. Spoon the cooled custard into the tart cases and bake for 20 minutes until the tarts are golden brown. Serve warm or at room temperature.

# Spider doughnuts

Real doughnuts take ages to prepare because they're made from a yeasted dough that needs to rise. My version uses a thick batter, which cooks to make puffy, spidery-shaped rounds. Serve them with a dip made from lightly whipped double cream and lemon curd, or cut them in half and sandwich back together with strawberry jam.

**PREPARATION: 15 minutes  COOKING TIME: 15 minutes**

## SERVES 6

300 g (11 oz) plain flour, plus extra for rolling

1 teaspoon baking powder

¼ teaspoon table salt

2 tablespoons golden caster sugar

50 g (2 oz) butter, melted

200 ml (7 fl oz) milk

4 eggs, beaten

vegetable oil, for deep-frying

icing or golden caster sugar, for dusting

## METHOD

**1** Sift the flour, baking powder and salt into a large bowl. Stir in the sugar and make a well in the centre.

**2** Stir in the butter, milk, eggs and 100 ml (3½ fl oz) water to make a smooth, thick batter.

**3** Heat the oil in the pan and drop in small spoonfuls of the mixture; cook for 5 minutes until brown and cooked through. Drain on kitchen paper, then dust liberally with sugar and serve.

**CHEF'S TIP:** Try to make sure that the batter goes into the pan as a dollop rather than letting it trail off the spoon in a stream – this would give you long, snaky fritters instead of round spiders.

# Lemon vanilla crêpes

You simply cannot beat a French-style crêpe with a sprinkling of sugar (vanilla sugar, in an ideal world) and a squeeze of fresh lemon juice.

**PREPARATION: 15 minutes  COOKING TIME: 15 minutes**

## SERVES 4 (makes about 8)

50 g (2 oz) plain flour

50 g (2 oz) caster sugar

2 eggs

300 ml (½ pint) milk

50 g (2 oz) butter, melted

vegetable oil, for shallow-frying

vanilla sugar or golden caster sugar

2 juicy lemons, cut into quarters

## METHOD

**1** Place the flour and sugar in a bowl. Crack in the eggs and gradually beat in the milk and butter to make a smooth, thin batter.

**2** Heat about ½ teaspoon of oil in a crêpe pan or small frying-pan. Swirl in a thin coating of batter and cook until golden, flip over and cook the other side. Fold each pancake into halves or quarters and serve immediately with a sprinkling of sugar and splash of lemon juice.

## FILL 'EM UP

If you feel like going the whole way, here's a couple of pancake fillers for you to try.

Mix together a 250 g carton of mascarpone with one tablespoon of sifted icing sugar (and maybe a splash of orange or coffee liqueur). Ripple through three tablespoons of ready-made chocolate sauce and spoon into warm pancakes before folding.

Place 250 g frozen summer berries in a bowl and sprinkle over 2 tablespoons of icing sugar. Allow to thaw for a few hours, then ripple in a 200 g carton of crème fraîche.

# Iced caffe latte cups

I've taken my favourite milky coffee drink and turned it into a really simple but very stylish ice-cream dessert. Make this well ahead of time, but remember to place the cups in the fridge for 1 hour or so before serving so that the caffe latte can soften and you won't be in danger of bending your spoons.

**PREPARATION: 5 minutes + freezing time**

## SERVES 6

4 tablespoons golden caster sugar

100 ml (3½ fl oz) freshly made espresso coffee

420 ml can evaporated milk

300 ml (½ pint) single cream

handful roasted coffee beans

cantuccini or chocolate finger biscuits, to serve

## METHOD

**1** Stir the sugar into the coffee until dissolved. Mix in the evaporated milk and single cream.

**2** Pour into six coffee cups and scatter four or five coffee beans on top of each. Freeze for several hours until frozen solid. About an hour before serving, transfer to the fridge, then serve with a biscuit or two on the side.

# Simple saffron kulfi

Kulfi is a scrumptious Indian ice-cream that is often flavoured with fruit, such as mango, or nuts, such as pistachios. I've kept this very simple by just using saffron but, for a touch of luxury, I've topped each serving with a sliver of edible gold or silver leaf, which you can buy in cake shops or from art and craft shops. You need to stir the milk frequently so that it doesn't burn on the bottom of the pan.

**PREPARATION: 5 minutes + freezing time  COOKING TIME: 5 minutes**

## SERVES 6

600 ml (1 pint) milk

2 large pinches of saffron

420 ml can evaporated milk

6 tablespoons caster sugar

## METHOD

**1** Place all the ingredients in a pan and heat gently, stirring until the sugar dissolves. Remove from the heat and allow to cool. Pour into individual moulds and freeze for at least 2 hours until solid.

**2** Turn the kulfi out on to serving plates and top each with a sliver of gold or silver leaf; serve immediately.

**TRY THIS:** You can buy special conical-shaped moulds from Asian stores to freeze your desserts in – they're quite cheap. Alternatively, save a few empty yoghurt cartons, wash thoroughly and keep to use as your kulfi moulds.

# Dad's
## chocolate-chip coconut cookies

Warm cookies straight from the oven are a treat few can resist – ask my dad. However, if my children have been really, really good, I sandwich pairs of cookies together when they've slightly cooled with vanilla or lemon curd ice-cream.

**PREPARATION: 15 minutes  COOKING TIME: 15 minutes**

### MAKES 18

175 g (6 oz) butter, room temperature

175 g (6 oz) caster sugar

½ teaspoon vanilla extract

100 g (4 oz) plain flour

100 g (4 oz) self-raising flour

50 g (2 oz) desiccated coconut

150 g (5 oz) dark chocolate, roughly chopped

### METHOD

**1** Pre-heat the oven to 190°C/375°F/Gas 5. Using electric beaters, whisk together the butter, sugar and vanilla until pale and fluffy.

**2** Sift in the flours, then fold in the coconut and chocolate.

**3** Shape the mixture into balls, then roughly flatten out on 2 baking sheets with the palm of your hand, leaving room for them to spread slightly.

**4** Bake for 15 minutes until lightly browned. Allow the cookies to cool for a few minutes, then eat while still warm. Alternatively, transfer to a wire rack and leave to cool completely. Store in an airtight jar until needed. Now, where's that ice-cream?

# Ribbled raspberry
## and white chocolate muffins

I've baked these muffins in parchment paper because it reminds me of breakfasting in continental cafés. Serve with a shot of espresso or a long milky coffee for a luxurious start to the day.

**PREPARATION: 20 minutes  COOKING TIME: 30 minutes**

## MAKES 8

300 g (11 oz) plain flour

2 teaspoons baking powder

150 g (5 oz) golden caster sugar

1 egg

1 teaspoon vanilla extract

225 ml (7½ fl oz) milk

50 g (2 oz) butter, melted

100 g (4 oz) fresh raspberries

75 g (3 oz) chopped white chocolate

## METHOD

**1** Pre-heat the oven to 200°C/400°F/Gas 6. Cut parchment or greaseproof paper into 8 x 15 cm (6 inch) circles and push, creasing the paper to fit, into a muffin tin.

**2** Sift the flour and baking powder into a large bowl and stir in the sugar. Crack the egg into a separate bowl and whisk in the vanilla extract, milk and melted butter.

**3** Stir the liquid into the dry ingredients with the raspberries and chocolate, taking care not to over-mix. Spoon the mixture into the parchment cases and bake for 30 minutes or so until well risen and just firm.

**TRY THIS:** Try making these muffins with other fruit, such as blueberries or diced strawberries.

# American dream pancakes

These lovely little pancakes make a great dessert or breakfast. Try adding some fresh fruit, such as blueberries or raspberries, to the batter, or stack them high and drizzle with runny honey or maple syrup and a dollop of clotted cream or crème fraîche. Oh, one could go on and on…

**PREPARATION: 5 minutes  COOKING TIME: 10–15 minutes**

## SERVES 4

2 eggs

5 tablespoons milk

150 g (5 oz) self-raising flour

2 tablespoons caster sugar

½ teaspoon salt

1 tablespoon vegetable oil, for frying

crème fraîche and ground cinnamon, to serve

## METHOD

**1** Whisk together the eggs and milk. Place the flour, sugar and salt in a large bowl, make a well in the centre, pour in the liquid and beat with a hand whisk until smooth.

**2** Heat a little oil in a large non-stick frying-pan. Gently drop large spoonfuls of the pancake mixture into the hot pan and cook for 2 minutes until crisp and golden. Carefully turn and cook for 1 minute until golden.

**3** Transfer the pancakes to serving plates, dust with a little cinnamon and top with a dollop of crème fraîche. Serve warm.

# Sophisticated
# strawberry sundae

They may be old-fashioned, but sundaes are such a decadent treat that it's time we saw more of them back in our parks and cafés. Here's the classic sundae, guaranteed to get you oooh-ing and aaah-Ing. I've made it a touch more sophisticated by adding orange liqueur to the whipped cream, and it's marvellous.

**PREPARATION: 10 minutes  COOKING TIME: 5 minutes**

## SERVES 4

150 ml carton double cream

1 tablespoon icing sugar

2 tablespoons orange liqueur, such as Grand Marnier or Cointreau

8 scoops vanilla ice-cream

### FOR THE STRAWBERRY SYRUP

500 g (1 lb 2 oz) fresh strawberries

juice of ½ lime

2 tablespoons caster sugar

1 teaspoon arrowroot

## METHOD

1  Begin by making the syrup: save 8 of the best strawberries, then halve the remainder and place in a small pan with the lime juice and sugar. Cook for a few minutes until softened and pulpy.

2  Push through a fine sieve and return to the pan. Dissolve the arrowroot in a little water and stir the paste into the strawberry mixture. Gently bring to the boil, stirring, until slightly thickened, then remove from the heat and allow to cool.

3  Whisk together the double cream, icing sugar and liqueur until it forms soft peaks.

4  Cut the reserved strawberries into halves or quarters. Place 2 scoops of ice-cream in 4 sundae glasses and swirl over the cream, scattering in the strawberries as you go. Drizzle over the cooled syrup and serve for a classic, old-fashioned treat.

# Banana splits
## with warm choco-fudge sauce

Remember eating these at your local café? They work best if you've got glass banana-split dishes to serve them in. If you have only upright sundae glasses, cut the bananas into four and push them into the ice-cream.

**PREPARATION: 10 minutes  COOKING TIME: 5 minutes**

## SERVES 4

### FOR THE FUDGE SAUCE

150 g (5 oz) dark chocolate

40 g (1½ oz) butter

150 ml carton double cream

100 g (4 oz) dark brown sugar

2 tablespoons golden syrup

### FOR THE BANANA SPLITS

4 ripe bananas

12 scoops of ice-cream

150 ml carton double cream, softly whipped

12 glacé cherries

50 g (2 oz) chopped mixed nuts, toasted

8 fan-shaped wafers

## METHOD

**1** Begin by making the fudge sauce: break the chocolate into a pan and add the butter, cream, sugar and syrup. Heat gently, stirring, until the ingredients are melted and well blended; remove from the heat, but do not allow to cool completely.

**2** Cut each banana in half lengthways and place in the banana-split dishes, pushing the halves apart. Place 2 scoops of ice-cream between 2 pieces of banana.

**3** Spoon over the cream, then scatter over the cherries. Drizzle over the warm sauce, scatter over the nuts, then push in the wafers and serve immediately.

**TRY THIS:** Traditionally, each split would be topped with one scoop of chocolate ice-cream, one of vanilla and one of strawberry – like me, though, you might find it easier to choose just one or two flavours.

# Angela's ribbons

My friend Angela gave this recipe to me – her Italian mother used to make it for her as a child. The ribbons are all different and look really attractive. Serve them warm with a fruit compote and cream as a dessert, or warm with hot chocolate for breakfast or before bed.

**PREPARATION: 20 minutes + resting time  COOKING TIME: 5 minutes**

## MAKES 18-20

250 g (9 oz) plain flour, plus extra for rolling

25 g (1 oz) golden caster sugar

grated rind and juice of 1 small orange

1 egg

1 egg yolk

25 g (1 oz) butter, melted

vegetable oil, for deep-frying

golden caster sugar or icing sugar, to dust

## METHOD

**1** Place the flour, sugar, orange rind and juice, egg, egg yolk and butter in a food processor and pulse to make a smooth dough. Roll into a ball, cover with plastic wrap and chill for an hour or so.

**2** Heat 10 cm (4 inches) of vegetable oil in a wok or deep frying-pan.

**3** Roll out the dough on a floured surface to a thickness of 5 mm (¼ inch). Cut into ribbons about 2 cm (¾ inch) wide and 15 cm (6 inches) long.

**4** Deep-fry for a minute or two until crisp and golden. Remove with a slotted spoon and drain on kitchen paper. Dust with sugar and serve warm.

**TRY THIS:** Tie the ribbons in knots, or cut a slot in one end of a ribbon and thread the other end through to make a loop; then fry as normal.

# Lychee, lime and cream frost

You can make this recipe with all sorts of fruit; you could even use a bag of frozen mixed summer fruits. For me, lychees are so refreshing, and the perfect way to end a Thai, Chinese or spicy meal.

**PREPARATION: 5 minutes + 2 hours minimum freezing time**

## SERVES 4

400 g can lychees in syrup, drained

1 fresh or dried (kaffir) lime leaf, finely chopped, or grated rind of 1 lime

200 ml/7 fl oz double cream

## METHOD

**1** Line a plastic tray with greaseproof paper and scatter on the lychees, making sure they're not touching.

**2** Freeze for at least a couple of hours until solid.

**3** Place the frozen lychees in a food processor with the lime leaf. Turn on the motor and slowly pour in the double cream. As the cream hits the frozen lychees it will semi-freeze into a thickened, frosty mixture.

**4** Divide between chilled glasses or bowls and serve.

# Clare's heaven lemon cake

I love a slice of cake with a cup of tea, and this is a really simple one with a deliciously tart lemon flavour. It slices like a dream too. Clare, my wife, came up with the recipe.

**PREPARATION: 15 minutes  COOKING TIME: 30 minutes**

## SERVES 8

120 g (4½ oz) butter, at room temperature

175 g (6 oz) caster sugar

1½ tablespoons grated lemon rind (about 2 lemons)

2 eggs, beaten, at room temperature

120 ml (4 fl oz) soured cream

120 ml (4 fl oz) lemon juice (about 2 lemons)

350 g (12 oz) self-raising flour

## METHOD

**1** Pre-heat the oven to 180°C/350°F/Gas 4. Beat together the butter, sugar and lemon rind, using an electric whisk, until smooth and light. Beat in the eggs, soured cream and lemon juice.

**2** Sift over the flour and carefully fold in with a metal spoon. Spoon into a greased and lined 20 cm (8 inch) cake tin and bake for 40 minutes until firm and springy to the touch. Allow to cool slightly before transferring to a wire rack.

**3** Slice and serve warm with cream as a dessert, or cool completely and serve with a nice cup of tea.

**TRY THIS:** Make this scrumptious cake a little more child-friendly by topping it with a simple frosting: sweeten 200 g (7 oz) soft cheese with 2 tablespoons of sifted icing sugar, adding a little milk if the mixture is too stiff.

Clare's heaven lemon cake

# Sweet 'n' easy mango lassi

Lassi is a refreshing yoghurt-based drink that's often combined with fruit.
Mango is the classic fruit used for it (use tinned if you can't get hold of fresh),
but this recipe also works very well if you substitute a large ripe banana.
Whatever the fruit, it's the ideal accompaniment to hot or spicy dishes, as the
yoghurt cools down the mouth far more efficiently than water.

**PREPARATION: 5 minutes**

## SERVES 2

250 ml (8 fl oz) natural yoghurt

150 g (5 oz) chopped mango flesh

2 tablespoons caster sugar

## METHOD

Blitz all the ingredients together in a blender or food processor. Pour into
2 ice-filled glasses and serve.

# Fun fresh 'n' healthy juices

Juice bars are springing up all over the place – in fact, juice is the new coffee.
If you've invested in an electric juicer, here's a couple of great-tasting, vitamin-
packed, healthy drinks for you.

## Stripy grape juice

**1** Juice the fruit in the order given for a stripy ripple fruit juice.

**2** Pass 2 green apples and about 25 white grapes through a juicer and
pour into a glass. Now juice about 25 red grapes and pour into the same
glass. Drink straight away.

## Vegetable patch

Juice 1 ripe tomato, 2 large carrots and a celery stalk. Pour into an ice-filled
glass, then add a squeeze of fresh lime juice; stir with a celery stick and serve.

# Fresh cherryade

This is nothing like that over-sweet stuff you used to drink bottles of as a kid – no, this is a fragrant drink that's really refreshing and fantastic for picnics and barbecues. Just you watch it disappear.

**PREPARATION: 10 minutes + cooling time  COOKING TIME: 10 minutes**

## SERVES 4

400 g (14 oz) fresh cherries, plus extra for garnish

50 g (2 oz) caster sugar

1 sprig fresh tarragon

juice of 2 limes

600 ml (1 pint) soda water

ice and lime twists, to serve

## METHOD

**1** Place the cherries, sugar and tarragon in a small pan with 450 ml (¾ pint) of water. Gently bring to the boil, stirring until the sugar dissolves, then simmer for 10 minutes until the cherries are very soft.

**2** Remove from the heat, then pass through a sieve to remove the stones and tarragon and purée the cherries. Stir in the lime juice, then chill until ready to serve.

**3** Transfer to a jug and top up with soda water. Pour into ice filled glasses and serve garnished with lime twists and cherries.

# Supercallifabulistic soda floats

Here's an old-fashioned Mary Poppins favourite. You can combine the flavours as you wish, but if you're using a fancy ice-cream, just serve it with plain soda water, and if you have a fancy fizzy drink, such as cola, serve it with plain vanilla ice-cream. Of course, you can always throw caution to the wind and try a whole host of wild combinations, but here are a few tried-and-tasted floats to be getting on with. In each case, place the ice-cream in a tall glass, pour over the fizz and serve immediately with straws for sipping. Don't forget the long spoons so you can reach the fizzy ice-cream at the bottom of the glass.

**EACH FLOAT SERVES 1**

## Cola float

1 scoop vanilla ice-cream

250 ml (8 fl oz) cola

## Orange soda

1 scoop vanilla ice-cream

250 ml (8 fl oz) orangeade

## Chocolate soda

1 scoop chocolate/chocolate chip ice-cream

250 ml (8 fl oz) lemonade

## Red berry float

1 scoop raspberry/strawberry ice-cream

250 ml (8 fl oz) limeade

Lemonade and vanilla ice-cream float

# Watermelon smoothie

Pretty similar in fact to a lassi (page 166), smoothies have become increasingly popular as a healthy drink. I've tried many smoothies in my time and this is most definitely my favourite. Like other juice-based drinks, this is really smashing first thing in the morning. An average small watermelon weighs about 3 kg (7 lb), but you don't need to worry too much about the actual weight: just use more or less yoghurt to suit your fancy.

## SERVES 2

½ small watermelon, about 1.5 kg (3¼ lb), peeled, seeded and cubed

150 g carton natural yoghurt

## METHOD

1 Pass the watermelon through a juicer.

2 Place 8 ice cubes in a glass jug and mix with the yoghurt; pour in the watermelon juice, mixing well. Pour into glasses and drink immediately.

**CHEF'S TIP:** I use a juicer but you can whizz the whole thing up in a liquidizer if you don't have one.

# Cardamom-scented
# hot chocolate and cream

There are lots of ways to make hot chocolate using cocoa powder or drinking chocolate, but the best flavour comes from melting real milk chocolate into warm milk. If I'm feeling really extravagant, I top each mug with a scoopful of vanilla ice-cream or a few marshmallows, followed by the grated chocolate. Total indulgence and a wonderful taste. Go on, get cardamom scented.

**PREPARATION: 5 minutes  COOKING TIME: 5 minutes**

## SERVES 4

1 litre (1¾ pints) milk

½ teaspoon ground cinnamon

4 cardamom pods, cracked

350 g (12 oz) milk chocolate

100 g (4 oz) extra thick cream

2 tablespoons finely grated dark chocolate, to decorate

## METHOD

**1** Place the milk in a large pan with the cinnamon and cardamom and heat gently. Break the chocolate into the pan and gently bring to the boil, stirring occasionally, until melted.

**2** Scoop out the cardamom pods and discard. Pour the hot chocolate into four mugs and top each with a spoonful of extra thick cream; sprinkle over some grated chocolate and serve.

Cardamom-scented hot chocolate and cream *with* Dad's chocolate-chip coconut cookies

# INDEX

Page numbers in **bold** indicate recipes.
Page numbers in *italics* refer to
illustrations.

## ACKNOWLEDGEMENTS

Once again, an enormous and special thank you to my food stylist and friend
Silvana Franco from Fork for her creativity, recipe tasting and humour. Also to Sharon Hearne
and Clare Lewis for their commitment and hard work tasting and preparing the dishes.
It was a real team effort. Thanks, girls.

Thanks also to my location crew: my series producer Sara Kozak, director Stuart Bateup,
assistant producer Vicky Jepson, researcher Melanie Stanley, production assistant Jenny Wright,
cameraman Alan Duxbury, sound recordist Andy Morton and editor Keith Brown.

I'd also like to thank BBC Television and BBC Books, especially my commissioning editor
Nicky Copeland, project editor Rachel Brown and designer John Calvert, Craig Easton and
Gus Filgate for beautiful photography, Elroy Thomas for standing in, my agents Jeremy Hicks
and Sarah Dalkin, and last but not least my lovely wife Clare and our very special children,
Jimmy and Madeleine... and my pet dog Oscar Poska.